Dear Dad -
perh [barcode] W9-DBG-938
we'll ~~both enjoy~~
reading! I
thought you'd really
enjoy it.

Love Laura
Dec 2003
xox

Catch &
Release

Also by Mark Kingwell

Catch &

**TROUT FISHING AND
THE MEANING OF LIFE**

Release

Mark Kingwell

VIKING
CANADA

VIKING CANADA
Penguin Group (Canada), a division of Pearson Penguin Canada Inc.,
10 Alcorn Avenue, Toronto, Ontario M4V 3B2

Penguin Group (U.K.), 80 Strand, London WC2R 0RL, England
Penguin Group (U.S.), 375 Hudson Street, New York, New York 10014, U.S.A.
Penguin Group (Australia) Inc., 250 Camberwell Road, Camberwell,
Victoria 3124, Australia
Penguin Group (Ireland), 25 St. Stephen's Green, Dublin 2, Ireland
Penguin Books India (P) Ltd, 11, Community Centre, Panchsheel Park,
New Delhi – 110 017, India
Penguin Group (New Zealand), cnr Rosedale and Airborne Roads, Albany,
Auckland 1310, New Zealand
Penguin Books (South Africa) (Pty) Ltd, 24 Sturdee Avenue,
Rosebank 2196, South Africa

Penguin Group, Registered Offices: 80 Strand, London WC2R 0RL, England

First published 2003

1 2 3 4 5 6 7 8 9 10   (TRS)

Manufactured in Canada.

NATIONAL LIBRARY OF CANADA CATALOGUING IN PUBLICATION

Kingwell, Mark, 1963–
Catch & release : trout fishing and the meaning of life / Mark Kingwell.

ISBN 0-670-04433-4

1. Kingwell, Mark, 1963– 2. Trout fishing. 3. Fishers—Canada—Biography.
I. Title. II. Title: Catch and release.

SH687.K55   2003   799.1'757   C2003-904994-9

Visit the Penguin Group (Canada) website at **www.penguin.ca**

The Fish

I caught a tremendous fish
and held him beside the boat
half out of water, with my hook
fast in a corner of his mouth.
He didn't fight.
He hadn't fought at all.
He hung a grunting weight,
battered and venerable
and homely. Here and there
his brown skin hung in strips
like ancient wallpaper,
and its pattern of darker brown
was like wallpaper:
shapes like full-blown roses
stained and lost through age.
He was speckled with barnacles,
fine rosettes of lime,
and infested
with tiny white sea-lice,
and underneath two or three
rags of green weed hung down.

The Fish

While his gills were breathing in
the terrible oxygen
—the frightened gills,
fresh and crisp with blood,
that can cut so badly—
I thought of the coarse white flesh
packed in like feathers,
the big bones and the little bones,
the dramatic reds and blacks
of his shiny entrails,
and the pink swim-bladder
like a big peony.
I looked into his eyes
which were far larger than mine
but shallower, and yellowed,
the irises backed and packed
with tarnished tinfoil
seen through the lenses
of old scratched isinglass.
They shifted a little, but not
to return my stare.
—It was more like the tipping
of an object toward the light.
I admired his sullen face,
the mechanism of the jaw,

The Fish

and then I saw
that from the lower lip
—if you could call it a lip—
grim, wet, and weaponlike,
hung five old pieces of fish-line,
or four and a wire leader
with the swivel still attached,
with all their five big hooks
grown firmly in his mouth.
A green line, frayed at the end
where he broke it, two heavier lines,
and a fine black thread
still crimped from the strain and snap
when it broke and he got away.
Like medals with their ribbons
frayed and wavering,
a five-haired beard of wisdom
trailing from his aching jaw.
I stared and stared
and victory filled up
the little rented boat,
from the pool of bilge
where oil had spread a rainbow
around the rusted engine
to the bailer rusted orange,

The Fish

the sun-cracked thwarts,
the oarlocks on their strings,
the gunnels—until everything
was rainbow, rainbow, rainbow!
And I let the fish go.

—ELIZABETH BISHOP

Contents

Acknowledgments

Angling, said Izaak Walton, is a brotherhood. We might better say that it is a community of interest, a chosen family. This book is about families both chosen and natural, and my thanks are owing to many members of the large group of people I am lucky enough to include in both. I have depended on the interest of many of them during the time of writing, sometimes more than they know.

The manuscript grew, in fits and starts, out of an article that was originally published in the *Saturday Post* section of the *National Post* (20 July 2002). My thanks to Mark Stevenson and Dianna Symonds for the generous space and excellent editing of the initial piece, and to Sara Borins for suggesting I expand it in this form. Some parts of the book also first appeared in *Queen's Quarterly* (Spring 2002; Fall 2002) and *Purple* (Spring 2001; Spring 2002). My thanks to Boris Castel and Dike Blair for their support. A few sections were also delivered as public talks, and I thank audiences at the Royal Ontario Museum, the Metro Toronto Reference Library, the Arts & Letters Club of Toronto, Humber College, Horizons of Friendship in Kingston, and Simon Fraser University in Vancouver for warm receptions.

At Penguin Canada, Cynthia Good displayed her usual infectious enthusiasm for what will, sadly, be my last book for her; and Diane Turbide did the same for what is, happily, my first with her. My agent, Emma Parry, is all a man could wish for in a literary friend and advocate, not to mention a charming companion for evenings spent in long-standing Manhattan drinking establishments. Angie Blake, Todd Ducharme, Julia Joern, Ceri Marsh, and Leanne Shapton offered encouragement, insight, gear, and good company. Julian Siggers gave me access to his enviable library of fishing books and expert counsel on dry-fly tactics. John Broere was an incomparable guide and patient teacher, tolerant of mistakes and generous with praise.

Some readers will be interested to know that Julian has a picture of a four-pound brown trout he caught on the Grand River in Ontario using a Tupp's Indispensable dry fly. I did not witness this feat and so cannot verify it directly, but I can report without qualification that it is a very impressive photo. And so, when I caught a fish on the same river, not quite as big but my first brown trout and first river fish, Julian was good enough to take the picture that graces

Acknowledgments

the inside flap of this book. He and John, who got me there, somehow conspire to make me look like a much more competent angler than I really am.

Illustrator Ross MacDonald, surely anybody's idea of a genius of *sprezzatura,* displayed keen interest from the start and provided just the kind of visual accompaniment this book wanted; it was a pleasure to work with him. Robert Hickey and Helen Reeves at Penguin secured permissions and generally made my life easier. Allyson Latta offered judicious copy editing. My University of Toronto colleagues Douglas Hutchinson and Graeme Nicholson told me some old and not particularly funny philosophy jokes that nevertheless proved useful. Molly Montgomery reminded me to look back, linger, and listen for Elizabeth Bishop as well as John Donne—just one of the many things I have come to cherish about her.

Finally, without my brothers Sean and Steve Kingwell, my father Gerry Kingwell, and the inimitable Fred Hawkshaw, companions of the original and now annual Weekends, there would be no book, and I would probably still think fishing was stupid. I had thought to dedicate this work to them. But somehow I feel that would give them an inflated sense of their own merit, maybe even lead them to think they can fish. Instead I will dedicate it to the woman who, in her different ways, loves us all: my mother.

Well, maybe not Fred.

Catch & Release

This Book Is Not About Fishing

"Angling may be said to be so like mathematics,
that it can never be fully learnt."
—Izaak Walton, *The Compleat Angler*

The first and most important thing you need to know: this is not a book about fishing.

Yes, it's true that there are some stories about fishing, also some fishing lore, in what follows. It's also true that I have shown some modest talent for fishing, following a somewhat rocky initiation into the sport. But I would be the last person to claim I know what I'm doing.

Same with golf, which also figures here and there in this book. I shot 103 the first time I walked through eighteen holes, and that seemed both impressive and unlikely, after the manner of certain sporting achievements that fall to the lucky fate of us non-experts now and then, with a fair wind and the will of God.

But I can't actually golf any more than I can fish, and I'm afraid you will look in vain for tips about how to be a better fisherman and, still more, golfer. There are plenty of other books that can offer those to you, and I urge you to consult them instead. If you spot mistakes here, which you may, and are compelled to mention them in a review, feel free; rest assured, however, that my brothers Sean and Steve have already noticed them and raked me pretty mercilessly. Anything I say about technique—even (or especially) when presented with an air of authority—should be taken with a grain of salt. Like all fishermen, I am a liar.

Even to call myself a fisherman is a kind of lie, in fact: a lie about lying. I can barely fish, would not pretend otherwise, and so hardly deserve to lie about it. But naturally the most accomplished liars about fishing are often the worst fishermen, and oddly, this stands to reason in the vast economy of exaggeration that Izaak Walton called "the Brotherhood of the Angle." To enter this strange fraternity—a community, thankfully, not composed entirely of men—is to invest in an infirm market of actual achievement ever threatened by runaway inflation, and actual fish are less significant than imagined ones. I find this congenial. Fishing, like philosophy, is erected on a foundation of apparent contradictions, the most basic of which is that you can't see that it is worth doing until you already see that it is worth doing.

Which is what, after much resistance and a few false starts, I came to see. This book is a sort of account of that revelation, an appreciation of coming-to-see. It is thus more a tale of enthusiasm and conversion—I might even say seduction—than it is about fishing. Finding myself unequal to the task of actually writing a book about fishing, I have instead written a book about thinking about fishing which at times closely resembles, without actually being, a book about fishing. Like many books, it is often simply about the act of writing itself, an activity that shares with angling and philosophy the qualities of solitude, quixotic devotion, addiction, momentary apparent pointlessness, and sheer dumb luck. And, of course, fabrication.

So, in addition, there are stories: lies with their good clothes on. You might suspect, with some reason, that the stories that make me look good and/or make my brothers look bad are especially mendacious, and that is certainly your right as a reader. I will neither confirm nor deny it, and simply say that some of this happened exactly as I describe it. Other parts . . . well, I can't really remember, and, anyway, don't listen to Steve because he lies even more than I do.

Pursuing this new, unsettlingly addictive hobby, I noticed a funny thing. Almost everyone who writes about fishing offers some version of these same disclaimers: that they cannot fish, that they are probably mistaken, that their advice should be followed cautiously if at all. They say: trust me, I don't know what I'm talking about.

This includes such incomparably good anglers, and writers, as the charming Viscount Grey of Falloden, G.E.M. Skues, and of course the insuperable Izaak Walton. It also includes the very best guides and gillies, who will lead you to the best trout runs, gear you up, tell you what to do, and then undermine any possible confidence with what I began to think of as The Universal Disclaimer. Guides are forever trying to be right without ever quite claiming they are right, then gracefully acknowledging that doing everything right often fails and doing everything wrong is sometimes exactly right. This must be frustrating for them.

On Ontario's Grand River not long ago, an experienced guide called John stood beside me in the cold, fast-running water of the trout season's first week and gently corrected my shabby technique, guiding me through a catalogue of faults, large and small, that began with a slack cast and included a brutally unmended line, a below-surface nymph fly running too quickly in the river drift, and a rod pointed somewhere between eye level and vertical. I had already put one cast in a tree on my errant, loose-wristed backswing, losing the fly in the process, and it wasn't even ten-thirty. "You don't get power on the cast if you let the slack run out like that," John said, observing me. "Well, okay, it worked that time." He paused. "Now mend the line a little, flip it upstream so it's not dragging. You'll never make the fly look real that way."

No, of course not, I thought. *Come on, Mark, get it together.* While I was listening, looking at the line, and berating myself, I caught a flash of silver and gold under the water off to the right and in the same instant felt a solid strike on the fly, which was flailing around at the end of the leader looking nothing like the larval insect it was meant to be. But fish are either very clever or very dumb, and occasionally both at once; sometimes they turn their noses up at everything except a random sudden movement, thereby confounding the entire universe of rational angling. Without thinking I flicked the rod sharply to my left and managed to set the little barbless hook. "You've got one!" John said, instantly more excited than I was. *Of course I've got one,* I thought. *Isn't that why we're out here?*

"Now let him run," John told me. We could both see the fish coursing back and forth in front of me, a large brown trout with the strong body and blunt head of a fish in its prime. I had some slack in my left hand and let that spool out, trying to keep the line taut, but losing the tension a couple of times. "No, not that way," John said. "Use the reel!" The reel? Use the *reel*? I didn't know how to use the reel. "Don't lose him! It's a barbless hook! A couple of shakes of his head and he'll be off."

I know it's a barbless hook, I thought. *I saw the fly before I cast it so badly into the river.* "What's the test on the leader?" I asked John. Would this fish be big enough to break loose? "Four and a half pounds," John said, and I could feel him silently add, *And you're going to lose this gorgeous fish any second now, if you don't start using the freaking reel!*

I was holding the fish tight and letting it run out with slack, still not using the reel's spooled tension properly, to tire the fish. Instead, I was playing out slack and holding the rod tight in my tired right hand. A couple more times the line went loose as the fish swam toward me. I desperately pulled in slack. The fish swam away and I gave him some. For some reason that might best be described as stupidity, I never for a moment doubted I would land this fish, and maybe that's why my variously compounded errors and contraventions of standard technique eventually won out. After ten minutes of clumsy battling, the fish got tired of me and allowed itself to be moved toward shore and the net. It was a lovely big brown trout, maybe eighteen inches long and over two pounds, and the only fish I caught that day; it was also by far the bigger of the meagre two our party of three managed to catch in some eight hours of fishing. That's the way it goes some days. Which is easy for me to say, because I caught the best fish—and before lunch, too.

John was happy for me and gracious as only a truly superb guide can be when none of his advice has been followed. "Well, that shouldn't have worked," he told me as I put the fish back in the water and waved beside its gills to revive it. "But sometimes the fish have other ideas." I contemplated this thought with great happiness at the end of the day, when, tired and sore, we sat on the bank of the river and I lit up a Monte Cristo No. 4 and took a swig of Talisker from my hip flask—which all anglers will tell you is the best imaginable way to smoke a cigar, the Platonic form of cigar-smoking.

The Universal Disclaimer, I thought, is the necessary standard dodge of all fishermen. It is the essential flip side of the exaggeration coin, intended equally to minimize responsibility when the fish don't follow the rules and ward off judgemental fellow Brothers of the Angle who might—indeed, usually do—take issue with some minute point of information or strategy. Much firm advice is offered, but the conviction in back of it is always ready for immediate surrender. This strange tipster's economy, far more volatile and ridiculous than a morning stock-market TV program, may be simply a result of the capricious object of our desire: "Theories, rules, creeds and hypotheses are constantly forming in the angler's mind," Viscount Grey says. "Trout seem to make it their object to suggest these only to upset and destroy them."

And of course, that deep truth, like so many deep truths of angling, is often enough forgotten in the heat of the moment that it, too, suffers self-contradiction in practice. This leads fishermen to blame their failures on one another rather than on the wily trout, which is very good news for the fish. Indeed, in darker moments, when a flurry of impossible demands, paradoxical imperatives, and half-remembered nostrums passes through the mind of an angler about to lose a trout, it seems part of the fish's devilish larger plan.

If you delve into the literature on fishing, it gives every indication of being a series of acrimonious debates over minutiae and distinctions of vanishing fineness, offered as if before a stern transcendental tribunal. Rivals are, it seems, constantly indulging in grave offences and then having the wickedness to commit them to the page, prompting a justified mixture of outrage and scorn from those better informed or smarter. And so one person's clever innovation is immediately derided by another as mere foolishness. There is no end to the arguments and no way in principle to settle on one truth over another, except (as Grey says) the basic fact that "always" and "never" are the least appropriate words in the thoughtful angler's lexicon. Disagreements over gear, weather, tactics, and judgement are commonplace. Fly fishermen, says Jim Gierach, "descend on the stream like information-gathering modules, sprouting collection nets, specimen bottles, and stream thermometers, and could often be heard muttering to each other in some foreign language I later discovered to be Latin." This is another way fishing is like philosophy.

Take, as an example, the celebrated dispute between wet- and dry-fly advocates, "a Lilliputian struggle" that occupied a good portion of the best minds of England at a time when, as one commentator has said, "Europe was blundering into war," which might have provided larger food for thought. But not so for the likes of Frederick Halford, whose *Dry Fly Fishing in Theory and Practice* (1899) touched off more than a decade of debate to rival theological dispute in intensity and outward pointlessness. G.E.M. Skues was the main opponent of the new breed of high-toned dry-fly magicians, and his *Minor Tactics of the Chalkstream* (1910) shows a mind perhaps more discriminating than wise. The dry-fly advocates—now considered the high sophisticates of the angle, often more satisfied with having elegantly caught nothing—were initially straightforwardly greedy: they thought moving upstream and floating flies on the water would catch more fish.

Skues considered this barbarism out of tune with the true gentlemanly spirit of angling, but he was engaged in a losing campaign. Dry-fly fishing has ascended to the pinnacle of the sport, not through success but through something far more typical: the mastery of subtle technique in the service of failure. It is harder to tie a dry fly, harder to cast the nearly invisible line, harder to lay the fly down gently, harder to get a good strike, harder to negotiate the rocky streams.

In short, dry-fly fishing *necessarily* puts wet-fly one down because it is more difficult to master, and therefore the odds against catching any fish at all are markedly high, just as fly fishing in general makes reel-driven spoons and lures look like an egregious form of technology-mongering, the hardware-heavy American football (or aircraft carrier) of fishing. Angling, like anything else, is about invidious distinction. It is a class system, and it is no great surprise that the Victorian/Edwardian devotees of the sport were responsible for both its highest literary treatments and its most fine-grained, exclusionary defences of what economists call "positional goods."

And so every angler since has been forced to confront the dry-fly issue, to decide if he is willing to attempt a place among the elite. The dry-fly fisherman is "the snob of snobs among fishermen," William Humphrey writes, in an analysis that might have been drawn from Thorstein Veblen. "The odd thing is, the other kinds of fishermen agree with him on this, and defer to him. They acknowledge him as their superior in fishing finesse. On second thought, is that so odd? The assertion of social superiority is usually all that is needed to make others accord it to you." The dry-fly angler succeeds through a "wonderful obstinacy." That is why other fishermen look up to him for catching not more fish but fewer. He is the high priest of angling, a kind of ascetic ichthyophant, wielding a carbon-filament rod and a tiny barbless hook barely discernible on a jeweller's scale. "His," says Humphrey, "is the sport in its purest, most impractical, least material form."

Thus do dry flies exert their fascination. Arthur Ransome even recounts a story of an angry bull that became enraged by the little balls of feather and thread Ransome was laying on the water when he changed from wet flies to dry, and that chased him through three fields. There are those who dispute the supremacy of dry flies, of course, as they would just as surely dispute any particular choice of fly or lure, any decision about rod or leader test weight. But there are still more refinements of the sport that take it farther and farther into the beckoning ethereal distance, disdaining entirely the crudity of even the lightest rod and most vanishing fly, and these are worth pausing to consider.

Trout-tickling, for example, the art of massaging or hypnotizing a semi-placid trout right into your hands, is for many the mythical *ne plus ultra* of the fisherman's art. It is dismissed by gear-hounds, naturally, who regard its advocates as smoke-blowing lunatics or plain narcissists; but whether or not you regard tickling as nonsense, you have to admire the purity of catching fish without any equipment whatsoever. "The operator lies down flat and gently places his open palm on the surface of the water, keeping it there hardly kissing the liquid," reported *The Fishing Gazette* in their issue of 11 January 1878. "Presently a gentle touch will announce the presence of a trout—unable, like a woman, to restrain her curiosity at the strange object." Right. Then all you have to do is gently slide your fingers along the calm body, close your hand around the gills, "and the trout may be hauled out in triumph, unless the tickler, in his excitement, has overbalanced himself and fallen ignominiously into the stream."

You can also attempt a literary variation of fishing without the mundane hindrances of rod and line, recommended especially for Scottish Highland streams by John Inglis Ham. "I recite long, sonorous pieces of poetry to them in a loud voice, bellowing into the wind," he says. "There is nothing that bores trout so completely—Herder, Milton, Spenser and Victor Hugo are the best—and they become quite distracted, yawn, and so make, for them, the fatal mistake." You might even want to experiment with methods of equipment storage. "Tear, then, as many leaves out of any novels which you may find, on perusal, worthless, or abounding with immoral descriptions," the Irish angler James O'Gorman recommended in 1845, "and fill their places with parchment covers, open at one end, and the full height and size of the binding of the volume—by these means, your flies can be made up tolerably large, full as large as the breadth of the book." You may feel free to treat the present volume in the same manner. It seems to me it is as likely to justify its existence as a handsome wallet for flies as to accomplish anything else. I get the royalty either way, so don't worry about me.

Anglers are, clearly, both superstitious and fractious. Against all odds and evidence, they are liable to cling to methods and arrangements that worked once, or seemed to, yet do so no longer. And against all counterclaims and even demonstrable success, they are wont to maintain positions and strategies in direct opposition to those of even their best friends. In this, too, they are like philosophers. But beneath the argument, the cut and thrust of dispute, lies that rare thing, a community of interest. Only those who are joined in loving a pursuit can disagree so vociferously; only they can convey their love in the form of a vicious internecine squabble. When anglers take issue with each other, accusing opponents of weak-mindedness or shady deception, they are really saying, *I love you, man*.

Just don't put your fly within a rod's length of mine, you bastard.

This Book Is Not About Fishing

As with fishing itself, this book tends to idle away periods of inactivity with peregrinations of thought and speculation. I wanted to convey, as accurately as I could, the space of reflection that fishing opens up for us. Hence the circles and idiosyncratic switchbacks, the memories and deferrals and long interruptions, that are set off from the main narrative. These interruptions sometimes meander, like the thoughts of the half-idle mind; they are related to the topic at hand, however, such as it is, in ways that I hope will be more or less obvious. They also abruptly, and appropriately, end when there is a strike and so a fish, a living thing that we are trying to deceive and, sometimes, kill. For fooling and killing fish is, despite Wordsworth's claim that it is a "blameless sport," what fishing is about— something even the dreamiest catch-and-release angler should never forget.

And yet, it would be crude to say *this* is the singular reason we go fishing: to put ourselves in the ambit of natural violence, to dangle and inflict death on this little scale, to return to our primitive origins as way-makers in a world red in tooth and claw. Just as it would be crude to say that any other single reason is why we go fishing. Such as: To bond with other men. To get in touch with nature. To feel the pleasure of the chase. To compete. To test our character and our patience. To step off, just for a moment, the treadmill to oblivion and refuse the quiet desperation that is most of life . . .

To say any of that—and believe me, it has all been said and more—is only to replicate the fundamental, if also forgivable, error of so much discourse about sports—namely, that they are a reflection, or a microcosm, or an accelerated version, or a decelerated version, or a prism, or a distillate, or a master metaphor, of life itself. Baseball is life in slow motion! Football is life at video-game speed! Boxing is life primeval!

But no, not really. All of these things are true, but they obscure the basic fact that baseball is baseball, football football, and boxing boxing. Sports are sports. And so fishing is fishing. Sports may teach us things about ourselves, of course, and we may use them to reflect back on life, but that is up to us. We go fishing for a complicated bundle of reasons, not all of which we understand. And when we fish mostly for sport—when we catch and release, rather than bag all the defeated rainbows and cutthroats—the reasons become more complicated even as the action becomes less pressing, undriven by need or hunger.

We catch and release thoughts and memories as well as trout; we grasp meanings one moment only to lose them the next, like strikes that prove to be no more than snags, or big ones that jump the hook just as you think you've won. Sometimes the harder you struggle, the more likely you are to lose.

I suppose that's the one and only sense in which fishing is like life at large. And all it really means is that fishing is worth thinking about because of the thinking that fishing allows. That is what this book is about.

2

Fishing Is Stupid

"O, Sir, doubt not but that Angling is an art; is it not
an art to deceive a Trout with an artificial fly?—a Trout!
that is more sharp-sighted than any Hawk you have
named, and more watchful and timorous than
your high-mettled Merlin is bold?"
—Izaak Walton, *The Compleat Angler*

I came to fishing late in life. That is, if you can say I came to it at all. Some men are born fishers, some have fishing thrust upon them. Others run screaming when fishing comes calling.

I enjoyed no early-bonding experiences fishing with my father, for example. There were no tense Brad Pitt–Tom Skerritt exchanges leavened by an afternoon of gorgeous casts and triumphant landings. There were no Papa-esque hikes into the backcountry to find idyllic wisdom and new insight about the place of men in the world.

No. In fact, the only vivid memory I have of fishing with my father when I was a boy is a pathetic incident somewhere in the backwaters of Prince Edward Island. Ordered to fetch a tackle box that we'd forgotten, I slipped on the bank and fell, cracking the lid of the green metal container in the process and somehow managing to get myself hooked and tangled in spinners and line to such an extent that I could neither move nor cry out for help. It was as if a malevolent spirit resident in the box had been liberated and emerged, hungry for revenge. Minutes or hours later, my irritated father, an air force navigator, came along and found me there, bleeding, immobile, and humiliated. One nineteenth-century writer suggested that the essential trait of a good angler is talent at philosophy, by which he meant an ability to extricate a mislaid hook from nose or lip without losing one's temper. I think of this early experience as an opportunity lost, but I came to philosophy anyway and fishing not at all. Perhaps it was because I lacked another important angler's quality, perseverance. I conceded defeat. The tackle box was bigger than whatever amount of character I had managed to build.

Since then, I have come across a surprising number of otherwise functional and well-adjusted men who tell similar stories. Wayward casts. Dropped catches. Snapped lines. Lures or spoons gouged deeply into palms, legs, faces. Also, fathers and brothers and pets mistakenly hooked. Eyes injured, tackle lost, lectures endured. We have been yelled at and laughed at. We are a sad bunch, existing without benefit of talk-show sympathy or support group, a scarred and bitter crew who cannot stomach the idea of fishing and, inwardly, resent the domineering, impatient fathers who made us this way.

And our only armour is psychic—namely, the unspoken yet firm conviction that fishing is stupid. Ed Zern speaks for all of us in his short but heartfelt memoir *To Hell With Fishing*. The key to fishing, as any angler will tell you, is *thinking like a fish*. What would the fish do? What does it want to eat? Where would it look? "Of course," says Zern, "the reason a fish thinks the way he does is that his brain is very tiny in relation to his body. So the tinier the fisherman's brain the easier it is for him to think like a fish, and catch trout right and left."

Or, as I would more elegantly express it, *fishing is stupid*.

I thought about all this as the WestJet 737 from Edmonton banked and rolled into its Kelowna approach, dropping out of the Rocky Mountain air into that gem of a valley in the British Columbia interior. The first officer came on the PA and told us his name was Brad, the captain's name was Mike, and they were very happy we were able to join them, along with Sheila, Carrie, and Steffie in the back. Earlier, the gate-check announcements had been careful to refer to us as "guests" and tell us that we were about to embark on a "wonderful" short trip to "cool" Kelowna. Employee-share-holder companies! Is there a manual somewhere setting down the rule that an appalling degree of informality shall govern their business? Or are they all just so darn happy to be up there in the bright Western sky piloting a superb slab of Boeing engineering in and out of the mountains?

I had a sudden rock-solid conviction that the flight deck was manned by two guys not only younger than me but also far more frivolous and high-spirited. I saw them arriving at the gate, clad not in the peaked caps and gold-swagged

tunics of average airlines but instead bare-headed and sporting brown leather bomber jackets of the sort favoured by the
Flying Tigers. Who could say that they would not, like characters out of *Twelve O'Clock High* or *Catch-22*, just decide to
start wheeling the plane around the sky in steep screaming
banks, whooping "La Cucaracha" back to us on the PA all
the while. I can even appreciate—in theory, anyway—the
frustration a hotshot pilot must feel when he knows his ride
is capable of a lot more manoeuvre and hijinks than the
boring bus-route up-and-downs demanded by most
commercial flight paths. I pictured Mike sitting up front on
the left, his hands poised itching over the controls, saying,
"Dare me, Brad! Dare me! I know this baby can do an
Immelman turn if we hit full power NOW!"

As with the subtle male passage of the early to mid-thirties, when professional athletes somehow pass from being
towering full-grown heroes to looking like they don't need
to shave, it is alarming when all the pilots begin to be
younger than you. I like to fly, and even prefer a bumpy
passage just so it really feels like flying, not just sitting in an
airless tube while some science-fiction technology moves us
imperceptibly from place to place. But I want the guy at the
controls to be a tall athletic man in his fifties with some grey
at his temples and the large capable hands of a former high-
school quarterback. I want him to be good at squash,

married with his kids in college—and a scotch-rocks drinker, but not today.

And just for the record, I respect and admire female pilots and feel good about flying with them; for preference, however, they should look like Julie Inkster from the LPGA, with the tanned, serious face of the girl who was captain of the field hockey team at Brown and then spent four summers sailing ketches off the Oregon coast. And yes, she really should be at least a little older than me.

Instead I have Brad and Mike.

Of course, I shouldn't knock Brad, or Mike for that matter. They are obviously superb professional pilots, pushing the big twin-engine jet over the corrugated Rocky foothills with grace. And I will say this for WestJet casualness: it keeps the crew from falling into the irritating singsongs, bizarre grammatical constructions, and pointless pedantry of the major airlines. Not for Sheila, Mike, and Brad the "We *do* appreciate your patience" and "We *do* ask you to remain seated until the aircraft has reached a full and final stop." (Not just any old full stop.) We are not told that they hope we have a good day here in Kelowna "or wherever our final destination may take us." (Dragged along by destinations?) Instead, there's a rolling stand-up routine.

"I will now repeat the safety instructions in French," the chief steward said. "Tak zee kerrd from zee seat pahket een frahnt uv ewe . . ." Another voice a bit later: "If you could give your full attention for this announcement . . . we'd be totally surprised." The standard warnings not to light cigarettes until well inside the designated areas of the terminal building were accompanied by good-natured joshing about the evils of smoking: "You made it this far, you dirty smokers! Why not quit today?" Even the pilots get into the act. On a mid-winter flight into Calgary not long ago, a Brad clone came on the PA and said, "Hi, folks. Jake from the flight deck. We're beginning our approach into Calgary, where the skies are clear and it is minus-26 degrees." Pause. "But it's, you know, a *dry* cold."

We landed without a bump in Kelowna, that plump smooth 737 slide onto the fast-moving concrete. As the plane approached the small terminal, I heard giggling, what appeared to be a girlish struggle for the microphone, and then Sheila said, "Stay in your seats, okay? Brad has to taxi a bit more." She told us a joke to pass the time: A duck walks into a drugstore and asks the pharmacist if he has any lip balm. The pharmacist says sure, and asks the duck how he wants to pay. "Just put it on my bill." Then the two girls at the front sang a WestJet song whose main feature is the fact that they are single and marrying them would mean flying for free.

We reached the gate without anyone rushing Sheila for control of the PA, the seat belt sign pinged off, and we filed through the door as the flight attendants handed us little strawberry candies and wished us a good day with apparent sincerity. "Have fun!" Sheila said to me as I left the plane— or "deplaned," as some other airline would no doubt put it—and I had a fleeting sense that she meant it. I like Sheila. *Hey, Sheila!* Her tone hinted that maybe I'd see her later at some watering hole downtown.

Kelowna is a great place in the summer, a pretty lakeside resort town full of good-looking college students working lazy summer jobs and otherwise drinking, smoking up, and having sex. It's like Banff without the attitude, and I would have been happy to be there if it weren't for the fact that this was The Weekend.

The Weekend was my brother Sean's idea, to get my father and his three children—his three adult sons— together for a few days of trout fishing, an event that, since its inception three years ago, has become an annual fixture. My father was pushing seventy at the time and rarely gets to see us all at once, we're so scattered around the vast North American landscape of professional striving and personal restlessness. Sean (my younger brother) is a restaurant manager in Vancouver, Steve (older) is an itinerant cellphone executive who criss-crosses the continent from job to job, trailing a jet stream of family, furniture, and stock options from New Jersey to Seattle to Boston. I'm an academic who spends too much time flying around giving talks and taking up visiting posts in Cambridge, Berkeley, or New York, looking, I suppose, for some elusive venue of insight or success, some philosophical epiphany or superlative cocktail bar that seems always just around the next corner.

So the logistics, or the odds of success anyway, were a problem. The family joke was that I would skip The Weekend in order to attend a society wedding in Paris, or maybe an IMF protest in Prague, but the truth was that I just didn't want to go. Every time I thought about rods and casting and hooks, I flashed back to my prone and defeated ten-year-old self, bound and slashed and sporting a dozen demon-tackle wounds.

At dinner the first night in Kelowna, or "K-town" as my dude younger brother likes to call it, I announced that I would not fish. My brother used to work at the place where we were having dinner, and our arrival had been greeted with voluble enthusiasm. Like revered out-of-town mafiosi, we were offered free drinks and off-the-menu food options, and a crew of youngsters—a dedicated harem of tanned, clean-limbed college girls with honey-coloured hair and volleyball scholarships—hovered around the table. Sean is a charmer, the family schmoozemeister, and he often has this effect on women. He's good-looking in a wholesome way, and now, in his mid-thirties, resembles Kurt Russell circa *Big Trouble in Little China* minus the moccasins and mullet haircut. Steve is big and jovial, the sort of guy who looks distinguished in a navy Brooks Brothers suit but more often wears the new transnational corporate uniform of belted khakis and logo'd golf shirt. They both have very short hair and look more like each other than like me.

Our father is a tall, substantial man, taller than all of us, and still handsome in a ramshackle way, though his heart and joints and eyes and teeth and hearing are all going in one way or another. It goes without saying that we love our dad dearly even as he manages to bug the hell out of us in varying degrees, not least for his heroic refusal to acknowledge any of the above afflictions except when it will buy him sympathy. The denial of his hearing loss is particularly funny or irritating, depending on your point of view and degree of inebriation. It means that poor old Dad sometimes lags a little behind conversations in a disconcerting face-to-face version of the gap that used to afflict satellite long-distance calls. His remarks, though always apposite, can find themselves slipping into the very recent past, attempting to board a train of thought that left the station a few moments before. We tolerate this little tic, or anyway let it pass without too much mockery, because, after all, he's been on the planet for seventy years and, well, considering the heart attacks and the gout and whatever else he's got going on, we figure Dad's lucky to be alive at all. On the other hand, sometimes we get mean and make it worse by using slang he doesn't know, the standard juvenile revenge of children on their parents. You might think grown men would be beyond such things, but you'd be wrong.

And then there's Fred, Sean's best friend. He is placid and quiet and seems like the quintessential nice guy in the standard Canadian mould, polite and reserved and inclined to silence. But more about Fred later.

With one thing and another, like flirting with the wait staff and mocking Dad, there was much incidental hilarity as we got caught up with one another's lives. It's not often all four of us Kingwell men are in the same room, and for the moment, before we had time to resurrect old grievances and toxic patterns of minor conflict, it was a straight-up pleasure. Naturally, the talk turned to the fishing we were all going to do the next day, and this seemed to me an unfortunate new drift, however predictable. By the time I'd downed my second glass of the large supply of Mission Hill Pinot Gris on the table, I was thinking: *You know what? Here's an idea. How about we forget fishing and just never*

leave this place. This is a very good place. How about we stay
right here *for the duration of the weekend and let the poor little*
rainbow trout look after themselves?

I will not fish, I said. Fishing is stupid. All that human
technology ranged up against the poor defenceless trout. Big
deal, you caught a fish. What now? Swatting a fly? Squashing
an ant? I will sit in the back of the boat reading Kant's
Critique of Pure Reason, but I will not fish. No fishing.

Despite my objections, I am ever a dutiful student. And I
had done my homework during the flight into Kelowna,
immersing myself in the wonderfully idiosyncratic literature
of angling. Rule number one of the seminar room: always
arrive with the reading done, especially if you mean to be
objectionable. As mentioned, it wasn't as though I were
entirely immune to the idea of fishing *conceived as pure liter-*
ary device, especially in its hilarious nineteenth-century realization, where the dangers of fishermen being "abolished"
by bulls or "harried" by wasps, those dangerous "creatures
fortunately infirm of purpose," mix with tall tales of
grayling, carp, chub, and trout landed with little more than
twigs and twine. I am as big a fan of Izaak Walton as the
next guy. I had read *The Compleat Angler.* I knew the story.

Fishing Is Stupid

Which is something like this: Walton was born poor in 1593 and enjoyed an unusually long life (he died in 1683). He is known to us today almost entirely because of *The Compleat Angler,* the charming little paean to the quiet fishing life that inaugurated a genre fertile enough to populate entire libraries. The *Angler* was published 350 years ago, in a first edition dated 1653, then substantially revised and expanded to its final form, the fifth edition, in 1676, complete with eight new chapters and a companion treatise by his protege Charles Cotton. Walton is perhaps the most famous fisherman in English letters, but in his day he was, not surprisingly, much more—as were most of his associates, the times being open to polymathic efforts in a way unlikely now.

He was a friend of Sir Henry Wotton, the scholar, diplomat, traveller, and poet who discoursed on diverse subjects, including architecture and the nature of political expediency. It was Wotton, sent by James I on numerous state commissions to Germany and France, who described an ambassador as "an honest man sent abroad to lie for the good of his country." His three criteria for good building, still often quoted, are "commoditie, firmnesse, and delight"; which is to say in more familiar language that architecture must at once house people or purposes, stand up rather than fall down, and be aesthetically striking. In later life Wotton took holy orders, became provost of Eton, and published his collected letters, essays, and tracts under the title *Reliquae Wottonianae*. His poem "The Character of a Happy Life," an earnest hymn to peace and quiet, suggests some of the very same ends of peace and contemplation that Walton locates in angling. According to his colleague Nicholas Cox, writing in 1697, Wotton favoured the sport because it was "a Rest to his mind, a cheerer to his Spirits, a diverter of Sadness, a calmer of Unquiet thoughts, a Moderator of Passions, a procurer of Contentedness; . . . it begot habits of Peace and Patience in those that possess and practise it."

Indeed, we may regard *The Compleat Angler* as Wotton's unwritten defence of fishing, for Walton is clear in the dedicatory letter that he is merely carrying out the intention of his dear friend, an accomplished Brother of the Angle who once said he meant to pen a discourse on the art but never got around to it. References to Wotton's technique—and to his robust, bracing character—are scattered throughout the subsequent pages.

But Walton was also friends with even more celebrated figures in the England of the early seventeenth century. John Donne, the great poet and clergyman, had met Henry Wotton while a student at Cambridge in the 1580s and was part of the London set that Walton joined. Donne's poem "The Bait," with the famous first line "Come live with me, and be my love," including a vivid romantic conceit drawn from fishing, appears whole in *The Compleat Angler,* along with the earlier ditties of the same family written by Christopher Marlowe and Sir Walter Raleigh.

Glittering, influential pals—also, somewhat dangerous ones. Walton wrote flattering biographies of both Donne and Wotton, and of the eminent theologians Richard Hooker, Richard Herbert, and George Sanderson. By his own account, he spent much of his life in the company of well-born clergymen—which sounds pleasant if dull, but in fact his life was marked by the very same conflicts and hazards that afflicted all those sympathetic to the Cavalier cause at the outbreak of Civil War in 1642 and, more so, during the ensuing Commonwealth of the 1650s.

Walton was necessarily familiar with the kind of daily violence that was a feature of English life at the time—an atmosphere of threat that would make most of today's literary types quail. Not every poet died stabbed through the eye in a tavern brawl, as Marlowe famously did—possibly the result of an argument over money, though some say it was a political assassination—but Walton's clergymen friends were routinely exiled, deprived of their livings, and imprisoned.

Wotton and Donne were both dead by the time war came, but Walton was very much alive and unsympathetic to the Roundhead cause. The first edition of the *Angler* was published the same year Oliver Cromwell dissolved the rump of the Long Parliament and was declared Lord Protector of England, while the final edition appeared some fifteen years after the Restoration of Charles II in 1660. Readers don't often put the book in historical perspective, so timeless does its simple message seem, but it is no exaggeration to say that Walton's passionate defence of the contemplative life is a mixture of apologia for the royalist cause and gentle polemic against the warfare then devastating the West Country.

Cast in this light, the book's opening dialogue takes on a new colour. We are told of a chance meeting of three strangers: an angler (Piscator), a hunter (Venator), and a falconer (Auceps). (In the early editions, there are just two characters, an angler and a traveller.) Each is a devotee of his particular sport and endeavours to prove to the others its superior merits.

The falconer goes first and then pretty quickly departs from the pages of the *Angler,* which is mostly devoted to Piscator converting Venator to the joys of angling. But before he goes he offers a description of the ancient diversion of falconry that is pretty convincing.

"I think my Eagle is so justly styled *Jove's servant in ordinary*," he says of that noble raptor; "and that very Falcon, that I am now going to see, deserves no meaner a title, for she usually in her flight endangers herself, like the son of Daedalus, to have her wings scorched by the sun's heat, she flies so near it, but her mettle makes her careless of dangers; for she then heeds nothing, but makes her nimble pinions cut the fluid air, and so makes her high way over the steepest mountains and deepest rivers, and in her glorious career looks with contempt upon those high steeples and magnificent palaces which we adore and wonder at; from which height I can make her descend by a word from my mouth, which she both knows and obeys, to accept meat from my hand."

To control such an exalted creature is indeed a special kind of thrill. It happens that I know a little about this because of a series of adventures coordinated, as usual, by Sean. I know this is supposed to be about fishing—though, as I said, it's not really—but first, following the example of Walton, a word about falconry.

When Sean and I first moved to Ontario from Winnipeg we lived with our parents in a little suburban housing tract near the intersection of Bayview Avenue and Highway 7, close to where the East Branch of the Don River forks again, in an area—not exactly a town—called Thornhill. Steve had stayed behind to finish his engineering degree at the University of Manitoba, Sean entered (and as quickly left, for a nearby public school) the Jesuit high school in North York, and I was in my first year at St. Michael's College downtown.

It was a long daily trip and my commute to classes at the University of Toronto was a two-hour public-transit nightmare. I eventually moved down to Kensington Market to share a big, drafty, cockroach-infested house with five other Catholic undergraduates of varying predilections and states of grace, but during that first year I lived at home. The northern corridor above Toronto was far less developed then, and it was a short bike ride to the open country of Major Mackenzie Drive.

Here Sean decided we should hunt for kestrels, or sparrow hawks. These little wonders, the smallest of the birds of prey, are killing machines in miniature, the midget class in the predator family. No bigger than a large pigeon, kestrels are perfectly formed pocket versions of the larger hawks—redtails and sharp-shins—still sometimes to be seen hovering and stooping by the side of country roads in southern Ontario. As with numerous previous enthusiasms,

Sean had carried out a prodigious research program, bringing to the study of amateur falconry a degree of concentration and acuity absent from his formal studies—a recurring problem with him. He might not remember any details of the Periodic Table or the name of the guy who wrote *Paradise Lost,* but he sure as hell knew where we could find the kestrels, how they behaved, how we could catch one.

Looking back, this now strikes me as extremely funny but also bold to the point of lunacy. It also strikes me, of course, that our parents, and our mother in particular, were tolerant and accommodating beyond all reasonable limits, for reasons that will become clear in a moment. I was seventeen, bookish and virginal and (I'm afraid) excessively earnest; Sean was thirteen and reckless. We were crazy. But Sean had, and has, a way of making you believe outlandish things can actually be done. From a library book he copied the design of a kestrel trap, which was basically a small oblong cage tied with little loops, snares in effect, of fishing line. The cage was not for the bird but for the bait, ideally a dormouse or field mouse. The notion was that the bird would see the mouse, stoop to the kill, and then find its impressive talons entangled in the tiny slip-nooses of the fishing line. The cage would be too heavy for it to lift and so it would be caught.

Which sounds simple. Sean had constructed the cage using pieces of tin-snipped half-inch windowpane fencing, wired together according to the illustration in the book. He thought about catching a mouse but figured buying one would be simpler. I can still remember the fall afternoon when he came to my bedroom, where I was lying on the bed in my habitual state of self-inflicted torture, reading Kafka or Camus or something equally *angstlich,* and told me he was ready to catch a bird of prey. He had tactics and equipment prepared. In addition to the trap, he had copied and constructed a hood and jesses for the bird, using bits of discarded leather cadged from our mother. The hood keeps the captured bird calm, and the jesses are a kind of leash, tagged with little bells to warn of approach, that attach around its ankles so that it will not fly away without guidance. He also had a thick leather glove for his right hand and forearm, where the captured bird would alight to be fed and hooded.

I was not so much incredulous as amused by all this. I couldn't be incredulous because belief or lack of it never really entered the picture. When Sean said he was going to do a thing, he did it, even if it involved hitherto unimagined expeditions, technical requirements, and new household residents. The family was used to, or at least well acquainted with, Sean's madcap zoological schemes and a manic interest in the natural world that today would echo Steve Irwin, the mad Australian crocodile hunter of recent television fame. (My niece Aidan, Steve's daughter, has inherited this latent Kingwell gene, to the point where she pronounces "snake" in an Aussie accent: *snike.*) There had been snakes and reptiles and other exotica in the house before. One captured snake had died, famously, by being run over by the power attachment of our Electrolux vacuum cleaner as wielded, presumably with murderous intent, by Steve, who later claimed it was an accident.

I had no vigorous expectation that anything much would come of this falconry caper, but I was bored—and curious—enough to allow Sean to enlist me as driver and backup bait wrangler. I got the keys to the family Toyota Corolla and we drove to a pet store in North York to acquire the necessary mouse. At five dollars it was more expensive than Sean had hoped, but we were too far along to turn back. I pointed the car north on Yonge Street and drove.

I turned east along Major Mac and cruised along the deserted road at about twenty miles an hour. It was a cold clear day with a stretched dome of blue sky so solid it would *clang* if you could strike it. The little field mouse was installed in its wire death trap, oblivious to the terror that, with any luck, we were about to inflict on it. And then Sean spotted one: a kestrel, fierce and small, perched on a power line next to the side of the road, lazily scanning the ground for movement.

I drove past and stopped. Sean opened the passenger door and dropped the trap beside the road. We drove thirty or forty yards on and stopped, and I thought, *Well this is never going to work.*

Then it did. The little raptor, having watched the trapped, frantic mouse for a minute or so, rose from his perch, hovered for a few seconds, and then stooped casually to the ground, talons stretched out to grab this easy meal. Only, just as he was closing that razored grip, his feet met the resistance of wire fencing and stopped an inch or two from the terrified mouse, a piece of live bait with nowhere to run.

The kestrel tried to lift itself away from the cage, but now the dozen tiny slip-nooses came into play. He was caught, and the harder he tried to fly off the tighter the snares went around his feet, the weight too much to lift.

I was watching this in the rear-view mirror, not quite believing this was actually happening. Sean made an inarticulate noise, jumped out of the car, and ran toward the struggling bird. Now what? He was ready, though, with the thick leather gloves and the jesses that would tie the bird to his wrist. He slowed and approached the bird from behind, enveloping its flapping wings and smoothing them down into its body. The kestrel struggled and bit the leather but then went quiet, and Sean was able to leash it and lift the entire bird-and-trap-and-mouse affair up off the ground.

I had by this time executed a quick U-turn and was pulled up opposite him, pointing westward and home. I opened the car door—Sean had his hands full—and he got in. For a minute we just sat there, side by side in the Corolla, looking at the natural wonder he had just captured. Seen close to, the kestrel was so gorgeous it was hard to absorb completely in one glance. You couldn't take your eyes off it. It seemed to glow at the edges, a compact killer: the large deep-set eyes, the wicked lean curve of its beak, the squat brown-and-white body somehow too small for the powerful head and big razored talons. Immobile in Sean's gloved hands, the kestrel had about it what I can only describe as a look of noble affront. It was clearly offended by the vulgarity of our interruption of its patrician occupations.

At this point we both started laughing uncontrollably. *Jesus Christ! We've got a bird of prey in the Corolla! Mom's gonna kill us!*

We transferred the kestrel without incident from the car to the basement rec room of the bungalow house where we lived. As usual, Sean was prepared: he had constructed a wooden perch next to the ping-pong table, a sturdy post of carpet-covered wood. He fitted the bird with its handmade hood and transferred it to the indoor perch. He also had a lure, a small piece of leather capable of holding some raw meat, attached to a string. When the trained falcon or hawk is hunting, you start by calling it back to you by swinging the lure around your head and, eventually, simply by whistling and raising your arm.

Now what? Well, Sean proceeded to train the little predator in the traditional fashion employed by hawksmen since centuries before Walton's time. First he fed it, pieces of raw meat mostly, taken from the freezer and thawed; this was done on the perch and then, after a time, while the bird sat on his gloved hand. Periodically Sean would unhood it so his presence and its indoor environment became more familiar. Then, after a few days of hand-feeding and acclimatization, he attempted a call: standing a foot or two away from the perch and coaxing the kestrel to fly to his hand for the chunk of hamburger or pork. Soon Sean had the kestrel flying the length of our subur-ban rec room, swooping beneath the cardboard tiles of the suspended ceiling and along the fake-wood-panelled wall, and landing on his forearm. On the other side of a small partition, the rest of the family watched television on an old Sony Trinitron.

Despite our collective nonchalance—eating our dessert over a Columbo movie or *Monday Night Football*—this was objectively amazing. Sean was actually training a hawk in the rec room! A small hawk, sure, but still, it was working, he was doing it; there was the hawk flying behind my father's head as he ate a piece of pie in front of the TV. Now, however, a fatal error. The point of all the indoor training is of course to get the kestrel so committed to you that he won't fly off into the wilderness. It's not quite taming, since no bird of prey is ever less than partly wild, but it's a kind of conditioned response that lies at the heart of falconry. As Auceps says in the *Angler,* a good falconer can whistle his bird back to the hand from a towering height; the bird sometimes even drops its captured mouse or vole into the master's waiting hand.

But you can't attempt this too soon. It's easy to get impatient with the long process of training, especially if you are a thirteen-year-old amateur with only boundless enthusiasm and a stack of library books to guide you. The day came when Sean wanted to take his bird into our backyard and start a series of perch-to-hand flights.

The first couple went pretty well. I was standing near the back door of the bungalow as Sean successfully called the bird the small distance of the backyard to his hand and then walked him back to the perch at the other end. But the next time he called the kestrel, it refused to come at first, sitting on its wooden tower and giving every indication of weighing up its options. Free food or freedom? It lifted away from the perch and appeared to go toward Sean, but then veered sharply upward and with a casual flap of its powerful wings came to rest on a power line suspended about twenty feet above the rear edge of the backyard.

Sean didn't say anything that I could hear, but he ran the ten yards or so that separated him from the bird. He stood directly below it and whistled to call it again. He held his right arm high in the air, the red meat clearly visible in his leather-covered fist.

The kestrel looked and considered. It sat there for a long time, and at no point did Sean break his desperate vigil on the other end of this ancient drama. He called and called, then, finally, simply stood, a helpless supplicant to his own desire and imagination, taking his place in the long centuries of men consorting with noble birds, loving them and so succumbing to their terrible powers of heartbreak. Tears rolled down his cheeks as he stood there, his hand held out, always held, aloft and imploring. The minutes lengthened and passed, the bird sat and looked and looked. Sean would not move. We would have to drag him into the house as darkness fell, we would have to remove him by force, lift him bodily, for he would not move, and the hand would not come down.

And then, after what seemed like so many wounding and awful hours, the kestrel, so lately captured, thoughtful and grave, opened its impressive span of wing and flew away, wheeling smoothly to the north and east, the bells on Sean's handmade jesses tinkling into the distance.

I went inside.

Fishing, says Piscator, is nobler than falconry. Among other things, its element is more basic. Water is the essence of life and though we need air to breathe we would not exist if not for the water that sustains our bodies. Moreover, the art of fishing is more ancient and more spiritual. Its lines are cast back so much farther, to Seth, a son of Adam, who taught the art to his own progeny, and images and metaphors of fishing are everywhere in the scriptures. The first simple good men Jesus chose to be disciples—Peter, Andrew, James, and John—were fishermen who would be taught to become fishers of men, while Christ himself miraculously multiplied the fishes to feed the unexpected multitudes—though if you ask an angler, that really constitutes cheating. The initial letters of the Greek titles and names for Jesus—Jesus Christ, Son of God, Saviour—spell the word fish, and even now the symbol of a fish adorns the vestments and collars of clergy, just as it appeared in ancient times on the walls of caverns sheltering the early Christians and their rites, a secret mark of community.

But nowhere in fishing is there the strange fraught relationship of master and slave, the kind where, as Hegel so clearly saw, dependence is mutual and ultimately destructive. You cannot exist as the master if not for the slave over whom your power extends; if that is so, however, then the slave has his own mastery over you as the underwriter of your existence as master. Power eddies and shifts until it is nakedly exposed as a struggle for identity that can end only in either destruction or equality. And since the falcon is both less and more than the falconer, a noble killer trained into compliance, equality is impossible. Every falconer is a lover caught in the ferocity of his own yearning, at once dominant and dependent; this is his joy and his doom.

No fisherman has this problem. Even in an epic battle between you and a big trout or salmon, the play of wits and guile and sometimes even brute strength, there is no sense of this subtle vulnerability where the very instrument of your sport is an independent creature. The rod is your friend, a piece of precision engineering, not a living, breathing thing that must be treated with the respect of independent existence. There is love and hate, to be sure, and a kind of fierce regard for the beast on the end of your line.

There is also the odd regard and irritation you develop for your own instruments, the rods and reels whose delicate perfection you must fear and master.

But there is none of the same kind of exposure, the same hazard of loss. A lost fish is many things: an agonizing tease, a spur to effort, a story to tell your fellow Brothers of the Angle. But a lost falcon is a devastation, a plunge into mourning. If fishing is an ongoing series of exciting flirtations, a never-ending search for the one that got away, falconry is a profound love affair that must always risk ending in woe.

Sitting in a tavern after a day of fishing, full of trout and ale, swapping song and story, Piscator and his friends sing these verses from "The Angler's Song":

> *As inward love breeds outward talk,*
> *The hound some praise, and some the hawk:*
> *Some, better pleased with private sport,*
> *Use tennis, some a mistress court:*
> > *But these delights I neither wish,*
> > *Nor envy, while I freely fish.*
>
> *Who hunts, doth oft in danger ride;*
> *Who hawks, lures oft both far and wide;*
> *Who uses games shall often prove*
> *A loser; but who falls in love*

Is fettered in fond Cupid's snare:
My angle breeds no such care.

Walton sees calm and rest in fishing, the contemplation of one's soul and character in the eyes of God. Angling teaches patience and grace, a silent communion with the countryside and its creatures. It also improves the health: at one point Walton suggests, in a passage that might have come from California rather than Hertfordshire, that a piscatory change of diet would allow his countrymen to throw off "those many putrid, shaking, intermitting augues, unto which this nation of ours is now more subject than those wiser countries that feed on herbs, salads, and plenty of fish."

Above all, fishing is an art, with the same combination of precise demands and complicated pleasures. "Angling is somewhat like Poetry," he says piously, "men are to be born so: I mean with inclinations to it, though both may be heightened by discourse and practice; but he that hopes to be a good Angler must not only bring an inquiring, searching, observing wit, but he must bring a large measure of hope and patience, and a love and propensity to the art itself; but having once got and practised it, then doubt not but that Angling will prove to be so pleasant, that it will prove to be like virtue, a reward to itself."

No wonder kids hate it.

But sometimes, luckily, late enough in life to make a difference, when enough time has passed and enough life has etched its marks on them, they get a chance to come back to it, as I did. To come back to themselves.

3

Golf Is Also Stupid

"We do not all care for the same pleasures, and do not
want to hear about those of other people.
There are even men and women who do not
care to play golf, and prefer to avoid the subject . . ."
—Viscount Grey, *Fly Fishing*

Catch & Release

The idea of The Weekends included a couple of rounds of golf bookending the fishing, and we had an early tee time for the morning following the first-night reunion. So naturally, instead of retiring at a reasonable hour and resting up for the links, we ditched Dad right after dinner and marched along the Kelowna boardwalk in search of happening nightlife.

There was plenty of it, though mostly in a form indistinguishable from a beer commercial or fraternity kegger. I watched as Sean and Fred shot some memorably bad pool—indeed, it had to be exceptionally bad for us to remember it, or anything at all from this stage of the evening, the next day. Then we switched up, and Fred and I shot a game of even worse pool, with scratches galore and cues waving around like playtime swords. Suddenly the place seemed full of loud Americans, all wearing rugby shirts and baseball caps, who took issue with our skill level, and we decided it was no longer a venue deserving of our custom. Steve peeled off at this point, claiming jet lag, a move the rest of us derided as a surprising and shameful lack of spirit, owing, probably, to his recent entry into fatherhood.

We were still shaking our heads sadly over this disappointing decline when we pitched up at a cheesy nightclub in "downtown" Kelowna, the sort of place where revolving lights spin over an empty dance floor, the bouncers are pointlessly aggressive while maintaining a non-existent line of clamouring would-be entrants, and all the women seem to have lost their way from a museum field trip for third-graders. We were drinking gin-and-tonics, reasoning that this was better than beer, after all the wine we'd had for dinner. This made perfect sense to us at the time but had the slight drawback of being entirely untrue.

A girl came up to the three of us and said to me, "I think you're cute. Do you want to dance?"

I glanced at Sean and Fred, who were looking at me with the blank stares of the bar buddy or party wingman, on principle offering no comment: *You're on your own, dude*.

"I'm thirty-eight years old," I said to the girl, with what seemed to me exceptional chivalry. Sheer age aside, she really ought to know that my best dance moves dated from 1982 and would therefore resemble, depending on the soundtrack, a Duran Duran video (step right, step left, slice the air with your hands) or an early Clash gig (pogo repeatedly up and down, not necessarily in time with the music or anything else).

She looked at me, rolled her eyes, smartly wheeled 180 degrees, and walked off without another word.

"Time to go," I said.

The next morning we floated, bleary-eyed, in the motel's little outdoor swimming pool, drinking system-shocking coffee and planning our big day. The idea was to drive in two vehicles out to the golf course, play our eighteen awesome, graceful holes of golf, load up on groceries and drink, then head up to the lake in time for some casts before dark.

I hate golf, mostly because I'm bad at it and everyone else in the family is pretty good. Even my father, who has been known to throw a perfectly good golf club into a water hazard after depositing three successive balls in the same place, can play the game. I, charitably, suck.

True, I did knock around a decent score my very first time out. And every now and then I hit my three wood or nine iron *exactly right,* so that the ball sings off the club-face and rises in the low ascending arc or sweet parabola of the well-struck golf shot. This is cruel, for the simple reason that it makes me feel I can play the game, would indeed be pretty good at it if only . . . well, if only I were any good at it. With the possible exception of ethereal talents like Tiger Woods, I believe all golfers feel this way. And I'll bet even Tiger feels the bite sometimes, especially coming off that hip surgery or when his swing seems to desert him every now and then. See him hurl his club in disgust after he over-shoots a green or sends up a spray of sand that fails to carry the ball over a sand trap's lip. Tiger knows, as we all do, that golf is designed to be cruel. It makes you think you can do it, then proves, again and again, that you can't.

All golfers compensate for their weaknesses in various ways. They ward off the effects of habitual hook by ruddering their stance around, like dead-pull hitters trying to get a base hit into the shift-opened gap. They select too much club to offset a wonky swing, reasoning dangerously that more power will cure inaccuracy. They play long irons to deal with wood shots that won't lift. None of this really works. Oh sure, it works *a bit*. Just about anything is likely to work *a bit*, and golf is one of those multiple-variable games where, sometimes, the crazier innovation is the one briefly most successful. Your unorthodox fairway-wood putts and massive pitching-wedge second shots seem to be working, or at least not not-working. But the game is bigger than all of our meagre efforts to overcome weakness. The game knows all about weakness. It practically invented itself to exploit weakness.

So here's what I do. I try to play irons from tee to green, no matter how long the hole. Of course, yes, this means I run into regular quadruple-bogey opportunities, which is less than ideal. On the other hand, I can usually hit the irons straight, which helps in not losing more than a dozen balls a round. And sure, it can be humiliating to tee off a par-five with an iron and play two strokes just to catch up to everybody else's booming drivers. But slow and steady wins the race, right? Well, no, wrong—in golf, anyway. But who cares? Also, I don't count as strokes the times I (a) fail to hit the ball altogether, (b) hit the ground immediately behind the ball, or (c) hit the ball in such a way that it whizzes off to the right in an angry twenty-yard topspin trajectory almost exactly perpendicular to where I am aiming.

Golf, in short, is as stupid as fishing. But I persist in thinking I will find a new level of success in the next round I play. I have enjoyed the times I played with just my father because we discovered, to our relief, that it was one of the few things we could do together without getting on each other's nerves too much—an experience I have discovered is common among the men I know. I like playing with Steve because he's funny, but he's too good. He's also the one who coaxed me onto a course the very first time, the week he was getting married, and I can never quite forgive him for that.

"Mark," he said, flattering me in his sly, evil way, "you're a natural athlete. This will be child's play for you. Besides, the club does all the work. Just remember that. It's all physics."

I always get alarmed when Steve says *you're a natural athlete* and *it's all physics,* since that is exactly the sort of thing I imagine Great War field commanders telling their ground troops as they send them into unwinnable battles like Ypres. *Ignore the fire, men. We will prevail. It's all physics. You are all natural athletes.* But for whatever reason, I ignored these warning signals in my brain and, gripping the club, addressed the stupid little ball.

"Basic principles of kinetic energy, Mark," Steve said. "Newton's second law. Force equals mass times acceleration. It's all in the club speed, hit and move, piece of cake. Nothing could be simpler. Physics, Mark. Swing easy. Keep your head down. Club speed. The club does all the work. No, no, *down,* keep your head down. Well, you've got to hit the ball for the club to work. Newton, Mark. Newton says let the club hit the ball. Yes, *hit* the ball."

We teed off in a foursome of me, Dad, Sean, and Fred, with Steve shunted into a laughing group of golf veterans playing behind us. We had decided, given my skill level, to play best ball, which is the sort of bastardized corporate version of golf that keeps people from feeling too bad about how much they fail at the game. Everybody shoots and then everybody takes the best resulting position and shoots again, and so on up to the pin. This suited me fine. I can make a fast putt now and then, and on occasion, given how often I use the pitching wedge anyway, my short game makes cameo appearances, so I might even get to make a shot or two.

Even so, there was pressure. "The hardest shot you'll ever make," Steve said to me when I teed up on the first hole that very first time a few years back. True enough. If the game weren't sufficiently cruel all on its own, golf courses make it impossible for you to suffer all your humiliations just among family and friends. The first tee is often constructed so as to be in full view of the clubhouse, the foursomes waiting behind you, the rangy, tanned scratch-game kids who park the carts, pretty much everybody. This seems gratuitous to me. I often remark on it, but nobody seems to care.

Steve's companions were the kind of burly well-equipped golfers I've always hated on irrational principle, hale slap-happy jokesters with merry novelty covers on their drivers and fractal-pattern shirts and ball caps from various manu-facturers of gear. They looked on sardonically, or so I imag-ined, as I pushed my tee into the ground and assumed the conventional bent-knee stance. Nobody remarked on the fact that I was attacking a 450-yard par-four with a five iron, my favourite club. I took a couple of practice swings that, as so often, had the annoying feature of being perfect, easy, and graceful. Then I held my breath—I know, I shouldn't have—eyed the ball, and swung.

It wasn't a great shot. Not even my most generous bene-factor, a person committed wholeheartedly to my welfare and happiness, determined to find the best for me in all things, could call it great. Or even, by a standard unmoved by charity, good. It was not a good shot. I can never get enough backswing on my tee shots, for some reason—oh yeah, that's right, *fear*—and this was no exception. But I managed to strike the ball pretty square and it popped off the club-face with a decent *thwok* and sailed about 100 respectable yards down the middle of the fairway. Nobody laughed out loud, which, believe me, is the main thing. Sure, Sean's big-wood tee shot went about twice as far. Okay, maybe three times. But who's counting? Not me.

"Nice shot, Sean." Always be gracious in defeat. It looks good to any pretty girls who might be sitting in the clubhouse gallery, bored out of their minds and drinking gin-and-tonics while their boyfriends or husbands are in the pro shop fingering graphite shafts.

We played on, the course was nicely laid out, and I relaxed into the rhythm of the game. Playing best ball, there's no real anxiety and you can actually have fun. I know it's not everybody's idea of fun, since nobody wins, but what the hell. Sean and I got to laugh at every hole, as our father, who can't see more than about thirty yards in front of him, cried out, "Where'd it go, you guys? You gotta help me now. Where is it? A little help, please. Is it over this way? C'mon guys." Sometimes we would tell him the truth, sometimes not, and for some reason, maybe innate male cruelty, this never got old.

On the eighth hole, I put a ball into the rough, and Sean offered to tee me up for a second try. He bent over and left the ball there for me. I noticed that it looked different, a little more matte-finish than an ordinary ball, but I thought, as so often when I am confronted by the unknown or inexplicable in golf, who cares? I addressed the ball, went into my spastic protracted backswing, and came down hard and slashing with the five iron. The ball exploded into a cloud of dust and fragments, and, as I followed through, I heard Sean, Fred, and my dad start to kill themselves laughing on the tee behind.

"The exploding ball, Mark!" Sean shouted. "The exploding ball! You fell for the exploding ball!" He could barely contain his mirth.

"Yes, Sean, the exploding ball." I felt like I was in a Bob Hope movie, or flipping through old issues of *Mad* magazine. The exploding ball. Hilarious. Were we going to order Harvey Wallbangers at the clubhouse later, engage in a protracted round of loud guffaws and backslapping? Should I plan a series of retaliatory old-school gags? The rubber club? The whoopee cushion in the cart? The dribble glass in the bar?

Sean and Fred were still laughing. My father was looking on tolerantly. What kidders! What a jape! My family, last repository of comic-book practical jokes. And, reluctantly, I started laughing too. What are you going to do?

My better-lucky-than-smart fifteen-foot putt on eighteen finished our round, we had a drink in the bar while mocking the fat-guy golf-bastard denizens laughing hard in that wheezy I-smoke-Cohibas way, then made our way back to the parking lot.

The trips to the grocery and liquor stores were logistical undertakings on the order of the Normandy Invasion, in our minds anyway, and we split into three fast-moving raiding parties for maximum efficiency. Popular cliché has it that men are bad food shoppers but in fact they are excellent food shoppers *if efficiency and speed are the main imperatives*. You can always count on men to emerge from the grocery store within fifteen minutes of entry, pushing heavily laden carts of comestibles. True, most of these will be in the form of frozen entrees, ready-made side dishes, and cheese doodles, and the combined bill will be in the order of $1,400. But food is food, right?

In fact, though, because Sean and Fred are such good cooks, and my dad and myself competent ones—Steve trails the field, except in the all-important area of grilling big pieces of red meat or fresh slabs of fish, at which he is the acknowledged master—we shopped both efficiently and well. The carts we navigated out onto the warm tarmac were heavy with impressive supplies of fresh vegetables, newly butchered beef, raw unfrozen seafood, and spices. Also cheese doodles, of course, because man can't be impressive all the time or women would get wise and stop trying so hard to be nice to us, and that would bite.

Sean and Fred were going to make the dinners, Dad the daily fry-up breakfasts, while Steve and I had opted to cover lunches. This was wise beyond our knowledge, since every good angler knows that lunch is the least important of fishing meals and can usually be omitted altogether. Arthur Ransome remarks in his memoir *Rod and Line* that the mark of a bad fishing inn is that it offers overly elaborate dinners and, especially, lunches of any kind, since taking advantage of the offered meals would mean giving up fishing time in order to return and eat them.

A good innkeeper instead loads up his guests at breakfast, hands over a couple of sandwiches, and is not surprised when the guests return late in the day, sandwiches uneaten, hungry for nothing more than bread, cheese, and local beer. "An inn that expects its guest to come in for luncheon in the middle of the day," says Ransome, "is an inn with a bad conscience, which knows that its water is not worth fishing." Exactly.

So I was all too happy to keep my good conscience, volunteer to cover lunch, and let Sean and Fred handle the main cooking. They are, after all, men who get paid to cook, whereas there are some people, possibly including my ex-wife, who would pay me not to cook. I will say again, I am a competent cook, but mere competence must collapse in the face of professional expertise. In the venerable tradition of critics and theorists everywhere, I did not think this practical handicap barred me from making authoritative pronouncements, both general and specific, about food and cooking. Indeed, it was at or around this time that Sean and I had the first round of the Great Osso Bucco Debate. The Great Osso Bucco Debate is a debate only in the sense that it continues to this day, and great only in the sense that it is driven by the sort of sheer triviality and bloody-mindedness that has kept families divided since before time. This is not my fault, since logic demands that there can be only one right answer to the question "What is best?" and it happens, through no fault of Sean's, saving his manifest error, that I have the right answer and he doesn't.

The question is, which form of carbohydrates goes best with osso bucco: risotto or polenta? Now, we're not crazy. We know osso bucco doesn't matter a whole lot in the larger scheme of things. It's just an argument about food—and an argument about food, moreover, in a world where too many people don't have nearly enough food to keep them alive from day to day, let alone the luxury to argue about what form that food should take. But you have to understand: this is me and my little brother. We don't argue about politics, possibly because we know they're too important to argue about. We don't argue about what happens after death. We don't argue about a lot of things that really matter. We argue about sports, music, and food. Things that matter a lot without really mattering at all. That, to me, is what brotherhood consists in: finding the things you can argue about without putting anything too important at stake. Naturally, this doesn't change the fact that Sean is wrong.

So: risotto or polenta. Now, before you answer—and I know you want to—you have to consider what rides on this. Osso bucco, the browned and stewed shank of veal, slow-cooked with sautéd onions and garlic, some chopped tomato, and a cup or so of red wine, is one of the great meat dishes of Italy, indeed the world. It's simplicity itself to make, completely delicious, and warm comfort on a plate when the wind is howling outside. In fact, serve it up to your true love on a cold winter's night, with some barely steamed asparagus, a good dollop of polenta, and a nice bottle of Valpolicella—a fire burning in the grate and Chet Baker on the stereo—and, unless she is made of very stern stuff, she will collapse on the floor from sheer happiness and proclaim her undying devotion. At the very least, there won't be any need to wear one of those goofy "Kiss the Cook!" aprons. Trust me.

The one downside to osso bucco is that it is made from veal, and you know what that means: these are the fleshly gains of torture, the cramped fattening stalls and brutal treatment of this suspended bovine life. But there are butchers who will sell only veal from farm-raised calves; seek them out and give them your custom. Veal raised and slaughtered humanely is no worse than any other form of meat, and there is no moral credit to be gained from refusing to consume veal if you eat other kinds of meat. As to that, there are many long and intricate philosophical arguments, most of them based on the minimization of pain and suffering. I will not attempt to address them here, but will say only that I am a meat avoider but not a vegetarian, and I'll bite the bullet on the morality of eating meat at all. I do it. But my feeling is simply that, if you're going to be a carnivore—and I leave that entirely up to your conscience—you shouldn't miss out on the world's great foods, of which osso bucco is one.

Anyway, that's not the Great Osso Bucco Debate. The debate is about why anyone would mess with the meat-from-the-bones perfection of the dish by pairing it with all that stock-laden rice. I'm not a big fan of risotto any time—it's fattening, heavy, and, in my opinion, like cassoulet or foie gras in that a little goes a very long way. On the same plate as osso bucco it's at best a distraction, at worst an unwelcome rival. Sean makes his with loads of melted Parmesan and butter, adding a new dimension of menace: an excess-dairy alert with heart attack on the side. No, no, no.

Polenta, by contrast, meets simplicity with simplicity. It's corn meal, just corn meal, made into a simple basic mush that can be found, per variation, in almost every culture of the world. My graduate-school friends from Central Africa made a version to accompany chicken stew, scooping it up with their fingers and sopping the gravy from the collapsing chicken pieces. You can find its analogues in Eastern Europe and the American South—in fact, in every place corn is grown and milled. And where it is not corn, some other grain, wheat or millet, may be ground and mixed with water to be one version of the staff of life, the sugar-loaded carbos that keep body and soul together from day to day. You can add Parmesan to polenta, and you can slice it and bake it into little cakes, but why mess with such an obviously good thing? It's best served straight up: mix with water, heat, serve. Maybe a little chopped parsley on top.

Sean and I don't disagree about the osso bucco itself. Not for us such pretentious and unnecessary adornments as cherries or olives in the stew. No funny sauces or tarted-up doodads. Just shank, onion, garlic, tomato, wine. *Basta*. But what to serve with it? There we can't agree. I used to think Sean would come around, sheepishly confess the error of his ways, and walk, head lowered, into the polenta camp. This has not come about, and we worry about him, since it shows a sorry lack of judgement. How sorry should be clear when I tell you that he even failed to be moved by a final, non-gastronomic argument in the Great Osso Bucco Debate.

"Sean," I said patiently. "Risotto takes *hours* to make. You have to stand there and stir and stir as the rice slowly, slowly absorbs the stock. Takes forever. You're a slave to stock, Sean! A stock fool at the stove, adding a few ounces at a time, coaxing the rice to say, okay, a little more stock, a little more flavour, come on rice, *absorb*. You're a rice lackey, a stove slave!" Even as I said this I realized that this was actually kind of impressive, a sort of puritanical good-things-take-time argument that now and then seems persuasive and in this case came down squarely in risotto's favour. Suddenly I had new respect for risotto. But then I collected myself and returned to the attack.

"Sean, when *your* date comes over, you are in the kitchen. You can't move from the stove. You have to dribble stock until the precise point the risotto is firm yet tender, creamy yet light. Then you have to serve and eat right away, or it gets gucky and stiff. The risotto is running your date, not you! When *my* date comes over, the polenta is warm on the stove, the osso bucco is melting slowly in a warm oven. We can sit in front of the fire and make out while Chet Baker sings 'Embraceable You.' I have total control over the kitchen, Sean. Nobody's running my date but me. We can eat *whenever we want!*"

"I'm not listening to you, Mark."

We arrived at the lake at dusk after a drive that mainly involved Sean telling me, alternately, the names of the birds his truck was startling out of the underbrush and why Dad is such a bad driver. Dad was driving the other vehicle, his big ugly pickup truck, so the talk flowed freely.

Now, I could tell you the name of this lake and where exactly it lies in the hills around Kelowna, but of course that would violate one of the key rules of fishing, which is that no information shall ever be volunteered. There are places everybody knows about—the salmon runs on the Miramichi, the trout streams of Montana—but other fishing treasures should stay less circulated. I sincerely hope you have lots of good luck as an angler, if you're an angler, but not in my lake, okay? Corollary to the secrecy rule is the possession rule: a lake or stream becomes mine, and hence not yours, the minute I catch a fish in it.

We unloaded the food and drink. Unlike the food shopping, our liquor-store stop had involved less efficiency, more dispute, and a far higher incidence of excess. The result was that we had two different kinds of gin, a bottle of scotch, some cans of beer—"For the boat," Sean told me—and lots of wine, both Italian reds and some tasty whites from nearby Okanagan Valley vineyards. I was reminded of a weekend trip I took to a lakeside cottage during university, when four guys bought and consumed over three days what seemed like a supply of alcohol sufficient to outfit an assault battalion on extended furlough.

Very soon I was reminded of something else—namely, that we were almost a mile above sea level and consequently prone to quick-time drunkenness. The booze goes right to your head when the air is thin, and people tend to forget this if their high-altitude venue is somewhere festive and uninhibited. For instance, I've seen thin women in evening wear keel over, hammered, from two glasses of champagne at the Banff Television Festival. There was also that time in a blues bar in Denver when I was drinking martinis with a bunch of crazy musicians from Cleveland and . . . well, you have to be careful.

We decided to get out on the lake, as planned, before darkness fell. We had rented two boats and a couple of rods for Steve, Dad, and me, though I had of course protested that I would not fish and therefore should not even be mentioned in the equipment calculations. Sean had nevertheless convinced me to buy a seven-day non-tidal angling licence so I could maybe, perhaps, who knows, join in later. Sean pretty much thinks of everything, which is what you want in an event planner, especially if there are no women around to make sure we do things right. His long pre-Weekend e-mails might have been drafted to outline a manned space flight to Mars.

I got in a boat with Fred and sat in the bow as he steered us across the evening-still lake toward a stand of dead pines in the water. He cut the engine and prepared a dry fly to cast toward the shore where the trout might be feeding on bugs in amongst the trunks. I watched him tie the leader and pull some line from his reel. Fred is such a good angler that he can spin out a beautiful cast even sitting down, a skill I have not come close to mastering. He pulled the rod back sharply and started the quick ten o'clock, two o'clock, ten o'clock motion of the textbook stiff-wrist cast, like flicking paint off a wet brush. The line payed out, spooling into the air backwards and forwards, longer with every tug, little twirls and curlicues appearing at the end of the line's graceful arc. Fred pulled the rod full forward and let the line unroll just above the surface of the water, laying the fly down with no more disturbance than the alighting mayfly it imitates.

An old question occurred to me: can something that is useful also be beautiful? More than that, can its beauty come not as a surcharge to utility but precisely as a function of utility? Like the swept-back wing of a jet plane or the sturdy upright posture of a suspension bridge, is grace here in fact inextricable from purpose, not a separate quality superadded to efficiency, success, and use but deeply inscribed in their realization? Philosophers are familiar with the problem. Kant says beauty exhibits purposiveness without purpose, a sense of direction without having any actual use, and therefore resists the reduction of itself to mere interest. Heidegger tells us that equipment—the ready-to-hand—conceals Being in its usefulness: we take up a piece of equipment, task in mind, without ever considering its existence, treating it as mere real thing; whereas the artwork, say, obtruding and insistent as the present-at-hand, has an ability to reveal Being, to open a clearing of truth. A piece of equipment may do this too, but only by shifting status in our view from ready-to-hand to present-at-hand—something that usually happens when its use-value breaks down. When I hit myself with a hammer, I regard the hammer, maybe for the first time, as a piece of Being, possibly even beautiful after its fashion, rather than a mere tool.

And yet, and yet. The cast is beautiful not in spite of its interest but because of it. Beauty here is not superadded to, and so not separable from, utility. And the rod's equipmental status is not overcome but celebrated in the beauty of the cast. The cast obtrudes because it works, not because it fails to. The result is, after all, a dead fish. I think: No, it can't be that simple, because Kant and Heidegger aren't just *wrong* about beauty. There's more to it than I can see right now. I have to think harder about this.

But not right now. Right now I wanted to watch Fred do that again. Beauty and use, equipment and art, thought and action.

Eventually, it was too dark to see where the casts were going, and we pulled the engine alive and motored back to the cabin, and sleep.

4

Who Is Fred?

"Success with pen or rod may be beyond one, but there
is the pleasure of the pursuit, the rapture of the endeavour,
the delight of an impossible chase. . . . Happiness in
these things is the legacy to us of the barbarian."
—Andrew Lang, *Angling Sketches*

Fred is Sean's best friend and fishing buddy. He is, you might say, Batman to Sean's Robin, if for no other reason than he has all the gear, the ultimate angling utility belt. Fred owns every piece of fishing equipment ever devised by man to aid in the uneven battle between twenty-first-century human technology and the pea-brained but feisty trout. When Fred unloads his truck, he looks like Arnold Schwarzenegger getting ready for the last ten minutes of the movie.

Fred is also, as mentioned, a professional cook who knows why organic baby arugula and kaffir lime leaves really are worth driving across town for, which means he is a perfect illustration of Canadian manhood, somehow combining the respective virtues of Ted Williams and Frasier Crane. This is a surprising, and surprisingly common, feature of the angling brotherhood, at least in my limited experience, whereby your grizzled fishing guide turns out to be also an expert cabinetmaker and accomplished installation artist with a store of allusions to (as it might be) Proust, Jerome Kern, and the Coen Brothers. This makes for delightfully vertiginous conversation. All during the Weekend, the talk shifted, without warning, from the standard male-bonding fare of bad hangovers and memorable rock concerts (Aerosmith, Winnipeg Arena, 1978; Tom Petty and the Heartbreakers, Maple Leaf

Who Is Fred?

Gardens, 1981; Bruce Springsteen, Joe Louis Arena, 1984) to discussion of the relative merits of Sancerre and Muscadet, the best way to braise, and where to find a special gadget for making spaetzle or cappuccino foam. There would be much talk of four-button suits, French cuffs, and handmade shoes. Then we'd gear up, go out, and slay some trout.

I have no idea if this conjunction of qualities is unique to this country, but I rather suspect it is. Unlike the macho versions of male bonding that dominate among our cousins to the south, or the elaborate borderline foppishness that can afflict the English, Canadian men have somehow managed to combine civility with violence, elegance with the outdoors. Hockey is of course the perfect illustration of this. The courtly cadences of the locker-room interview, showing some charming boy from Saskatoon with a scar across his nose, who would not dream of saying anything too challenging, let alone talking trash in the high-octane style of NBA or NFL stars, give way to him heading out onto the ice to body-slam and pummel his opponent until they are both bleeding. Hockey, like rugby before it, is a game of licensed mayhem engaged in by gentlemen. This is the politeness of good manners instilled by generations of parents who don't want their children to be overly insistent or mouthy but still want them to look after themselves in the pocket. Say what you like about Canadian character and its penchant for self-abnegation, this combination of considerateness and backbone is both appealing and manly, however incomprehensible it may be to our more aggressive neighbours, who just tend to think that all Canadian men are gay.

On that score, you have to grant, now and then, that they have a point, at least on the level of appearances. In the beer store on the way up to the lake, I observed the two burly employees out front who, in their flannel shirts and jeans, were the very picture of stereotypical Bob-and-Doug Canuck manhood, with a dash of frat-boy stubble and insult-as-bonhomie thrown in. But after they had mocked each other's inadequacies for a few minutes while I was waiting in line, this was the crucial exchange:

Burly frat boy 1: "Jeff says we don't want to hang out with him any more."

Burly frat boy 2: "Oh, he's such a drama queen. I'm not getting involved."

Burly frat boy 1: "But do you think he's upset?"

Burly frat boy 2: "Ask him yourself."

Burly frat boy 1: (going back into the warehouse) "Hey, Jeff. Hey, drama queen! Stop *sulking*."

Who Is Fred?

Now, I can't be absolutely sure, but I'd be willing to lay down some good money that the average beer-store employee in the United States doesn't know, let alone habitually use, the expression "drama queen," especially with reference to a fellow beer-store employee. And especially if the occasion for using it is the other beer-store employee being "upset" because his friends don't want to hang out with him any more. And even more especially as a way of "not getting involved" with his "sulking."

Be that as it may, on the whole the weird conjunction of manliness and dandyism to be found among Canadian males—what style writers have lately called "metrosexuality"—is to be celebrated, not least because it means that it's okay to know about wine, how to tie different kinds of necktie knots, and how to cook a meal more elaborate than Kraft Dinner. Not that I have anything against Kraft Dinner, because who could?

It's a fine thing, of course, because just a little too much interest takes these preoccupations from elegant to unseemly. Not very far away from justifiable attention to detail and celebration of food, for instance, is the lifestyle pornography of the materially rich and mentally impoverished. Eating out and decorating are wonderful things, for those who can afford them, but they quickly become the least taxing and most obnoxious forms of aesthetic preoccupation.

This vapid, striving sophistication requires little effort yet yields great rewards in ostentatious superïority. Invidious distinction is not just inevitable, but the main point. Such pursuits may also, even more seductively than the widely demonized dangers of television, take us away from important inward forms of recreation, such as reading, where we consider not just self-presentation but self-improvement. I suppose the end-game of this seduction would be the seemingly endless array of cooking and decorating shows *on television*. Suddenly, reading is a pleasure with too few ostensible-use payoffs, too many private costs for the realized social benefits.

And North Americans are doing less and less reading all the time, as newspaper reports tell us over and over. The difference lately is that the emphasis has shifted, and routine expressions of misgiving or embarrassment are now countered by assertions that this or that person is simply too busy, too harried, or just too *interesting*, to read books: as so often elsewhere, shame is replaced by aggressive self-regard. Where before a lack of literate interest was regarded as a fault, nowadays we hear people express pride in their unwillingness to read for pleasure, the way teenagers report themselves proud of being easily bored. And so, having asked a publishing executive friend whether he would rather eat out or read, one newspaper reporter got the following near-parody reply: "To me," said the publisher, "that's laughable. Charlie Trotter's restaurant in Chicago, an eight-course tasting menu, Chambolle-Musigny *premier cru,* every course to die for, constant discussions about the ingredients and the reductions in each dish—there's nothing I'd rather be doing. Eating is hedonistic. Reading is ascetic and solitary."

There is something depressing and ugly about such an assertion of bland complacency, especially coming from a *publishing executive*—to say nothing of the egregious use of "to die for," a phrase which should have been allowed a quiet death in 1993. But this, it seems to me, is precisely what happens when genuine aesthetic endeavours get out of hand; when people find themselves with more money than sense, and more interest in taste than wisdom. And yet, well-heeled vulgarity is the merely irritating surface problem; far more damaging is the insidious idea that reading is just one form of leisure choice among many, a low-level option commanding, at best, a mild pull on one's attention. Reading is solitary, to be sure, but that is its great virtue, and only a fool with no interior life could count that against it. The idea that reading is ascetic, meanwhile, could not be entertained except by someone who has never felt the lush, complicated pleasures of reading—the sort of person who, apparently, ends up as a publishing executive. When you see it that way, a lot of other things, unfortunately, make sense.

Of course, you knew I would say that, since here we are, you and I, two devotees of the book, immersed in the strange space of reading, where my words are sounding inside your head. This is a book, after all, which I have obviously written in the hope that you will read it, rather than (for now, anyway) going out for dinner. The greatest part of the manifold pleasure of writing lies in that hope for engagement, which, like all profound desires, subtly annihilates the very distinction between reflection and action that has dogged the West since Aristotle. Reading and writing are forms of action that show no outward exertion, that appear becalmed. And yet, reflection is its own kind of exertion, an activity that exercises the mind and the soul, tracing the limits of consciousness. It makes other actions possible, and, as we shall see, this is surely what Aristotle meant when he said, paradoxically, that reflection was the highest part of the active life.

Why dwell on this here, in a book of fishing tales? Well, because writing and fishing, it seems to me, share this transcendental ability to heal the breach between thought and deed, to bridge the world of imagination and the so-called "real" one. They share, too, by the same token, a sublime combination of solitude and implied community, willed aloneness in the service of something much larger, a sense of belonging. Also, not least, in my experience writers and anglers both tend to end the productive part of the day with drinking and backchat.

A large part of the pleasure of fishing is immersion, during the long winter months of fly-tying and dreaming, in the great shelves of literature written about it. No other sporting activity except maybe baseball has inspired so much, and such good, literary contemplation. (I leave aside golf, mainly because as far as I'm concerned it's still stupid and will remain so until I shoot 103 again, and believe me that will not happen on this mortal plane without some form of divine intervention.) And contemplation, too, is a form of necessary recreation. I don't mean the elevation of one part of life into a lifestyle choice—the conspicuous consumption, as it were, of one's own sophistication. I mean, rather, the simpler and more basic restoration of a state of native receptivity; an inward clearing of concerns and anxieties and even self, so that deeper thoughts may, in the silence of a lonely river or lake, softly enter.

Izaak Walton himself was no slouch when it came to recipes and directions for the preparation of fish, on which

Who Is Fred?

ubject he was a Friend of Martha well before the fact. He
never lets the details outweigh the main event, however,
which is the simple satisfaction of catching a wily fat trout
or chub that one will later eat. The thoughts that matter
happen not conspicuously, and not by way of consumption.
It's always good to know how to find fresh mangoes or new-
ground coriander, to secure supplies of prosciutto di parma
or real balsamic vinegar. But it's always better to remember
where these things stand in the scalar universe of signifi-
cance. When food, or any other aspect of living with style,
becomes porn, then, like sexual porn before it, it under-
mines the foundation of its own merit. It is, finally, possible
to be *too interested* in something interesting.

I suppose I also mean there's something unmanly, as well
as unseemly, about *excessive* attention to detail in
comestibles or dress. Dandyism, to my mind, is about
looking extremely elegant without drawing particular attention to what went into making you so. The critic Hugo
Williams, writing of his well-dressed father, notes how one
scale of value can influence another. "I always imagined my
father's many suits were proof of his superior wit," he says.
But elegance in attire is a tightrope walk, one that English
men of a certain stripe are forever claiming they alone have
mastered: "My father used to say you should be with
someone a full minute before you realized they were well

dressed, but he shouldn't really have had any opinion on th
subject. When I asked him what it meant if you realize
before that, he said they were probably queer." Williams
own "hyper self-consciousness" about appearance was, h
says, "fed by my parents' rigidly adhered-to value system
which placed only good manners above the all-importan
good looks, and that not very convincingly. 'Such a nic
young man,' my mother used to say, 'so good looking.' I
was the kind of judgement that bred a certain fatalism abou
life. After all, this was an area where human will was power
less to effect much change. I searched my face for signs o
excellence."

If fatalism and charges of homosexuality are the Scyll
and Charybdis of dressing well—in England, anyway—n
wonder so many men quail at the prospect of buying a suit
Manly elegance is obviously a hard standard to reach, an
en route we are likely to go astray. Cary Grant once said
"Every man wants to look like Cary Grant. *I* want to loo
like Cary Grant." The cinematic version of Grant, the Gran
icon, at once combines the virtues of style and manliness, o
suavity and physical courage. It's not for nothing that *Nort*
by Northwest is his, and Hitchcock's, most satisfying film. It
narrative offers the revelation that an apparently superficia
and even sissified Madison Avenue trickster is in fact a mar
of action and grace, a mannequin turned resourceful an

bold. There are women of my acquaintance, maybe of yours, who claim to find Grant too "femmy," but that bespeaks only a desire for rough trade that they should perhaps examine more closely. If Cary Grant isn't man enough for you, there's something wrong with your picture of manhood.

In any case the bottom line is style, that indefinable thing that distinguishes a thing merely done from a thing done well. Style originally referred to writing, the way one wielded a pen or stylus, and that sense of literary or calligraphical uniqueness persists. (If you lend your fountain pen to another person, their style will likely ruin the expensive gold nib you have over time carved to your own.) But by style we surely mean more than simply a discernible uniqueness in application. We mean the quality of apparent ease that marks off the person of accomplishment from the mere journeyman, the master from the apprentice. And this, it seems to me, lies deep in the heart of all forms of accomplishment that compel our attention, the desire not simply to do things but to do them with flair. Indeed, there is one of those pleasing etymological traces left here in the language of graceful achievement, the *virtuoso* performance, with its overtones of *virtus*, strength or capacity to act, and even more basically of *vir*, or man. There can of course be female virtuosos, but the language we use to praise them is nevertheless rooted in the unequal regard of men for each other.

Perfected from the days of the Renaissance courtiers and evident even earlier in the courtly pursuits and aristocratic qualities of ancient Greece, Rome, and Persia, the quality we seek is *sprezzatura:* that happily untranslatable Italian word that means, among other things, the ability to make difficult things look easy. "A certain fine careless-ness," one writer puts it, in praise of Baldassare Castiglione and his treatise on refined behaviour, *The Book of the Courtier.* "Grace" doesn't quite capture its extension, though part of it. Not "elegance," either, though again it is partly right. Vitality and lightness are implied, but *sprezzatura* is more than gaiety. It is that exhibition of relaxed compe-tence, almost of insouciance, in amateur pursuit of one's goals. A kind of social facility or comfort, an ability to find oneself at home in a variety of settings. Refinement, with its implication of a thing done again, embellished or polished past the point of bare utility—to *re-fine* is to finish again—captures the sublime conjunction of use and ornament. We add the grace notes and unnecessary flourishes the Greeks called *parerga*—literally, marginal decorations intended to beautify and enhance the main, useful thing—and again we hear in *decoration* itself another echo still, of *decorum* with its sense of graceful rightness, the appropriateness that marks the well-done thing.

But enough linguistics. Puritanical critics tend to regard *sprezzatura* as a suspect quality, a polish in manners that indicates overrefinement or even feyness, the transparent self-justification of the fop. But such judgements ignore the real edge that must remain beneath the polish. Castiglione's elegant courtiers or the dandy Cavalier poets of Walton's own time were anything but fey. They were brave, wily, and often dangerous men—men who served with distinction in battles and intrigues. Like the dandies of the early Royal Navy or the strutting officers of the Household Guards, these men were as courageous as they were refined in dress and comportment. Only a clod could fail to be impressed by the combination of poetry and military distinction observable in Richard Lovelace or Sir John Suckling. And yet, what military man today would dare admit he read poetry, let alone composed it? On the other side, from what poet could we expect to see a display of manly vigour, except perhaps in the vulgar form of drunken brawling at a book launch? There may be such men out there—I really hope there are—but no one could reasonably argue that they form our currently dominant notion of masculine accomplishment.

If the elegant side of this conjunction is nowadays poorly regarded, the side of physical courage is more

openly celebrated, the standard gauge of merit among men
but often with little reflection. Certainly far less than the
men of earlier generations, who lived in closer proximity to
everyday violence, brought to the subject. We do not ask
ourselves the hard questions. For instance: How much of
courage in the traditional sense, physical courage as the
triumph over fear, is actually reducible to the belief in one's
ability to *take* the pain should it come? It's not something
most men talk about, even with each other, and yet I think
we all wonder about our ability to withstand pain. It's intimately related to our capacity for violence, after all, both
committed and observed. Past the age of about twelve
however, it ceases to be a topic of daily conversation. After
that, the issue mostly retreats to the arena of silent reflection
where one watches a war movie or boxing match, or a football game, and wonders, *Could I hack that?* Hard to know,
since most of what we experience is more in the nature of
what doctors prefer to call *discomfort,* not pain, that difference between cash and credit when it comes to unwelcome
excitation of the nervous system. Few of us know real
physical pain until it is too late for us to make much use
of the knowledge.

Death is not painful, only dying is—and then not
always. Young men and philosophers alike see this, for
neither of them fear death—the one from a belief in their

own immortality and the other from a reasoned belief that death is something about which we know nothing. But though those forms of belief pass for courage, they are not. Courage is too often misunderstood: it is not overcoming the fear of death but rather mastering the fear of future suffering. It's instructive to listen to twelve-year-old boys talk about courage, therefore, simply because they so closely resemble, as Benjamin Jowett argued, the heroes of *The Aeneid* and *The Odyssey*. They are fractious, bold, touchy about honour, and obsessed with the relative toughness of their companions. They are deeply impressed with small victories established against pain, and as deeply ashamed of their own failures and descents into weeping. Like Myrmidons or Klingons, they live to do battle and die a thousand deaths when they fall short of their own lofty standards of virtue and character—words that, like *heart,* are still the shorthand in the sporting world for the willingness to stand in and take a beating. *He has a lot of character, that guy. He has heart.* Oddly enough, it used to be the liver, or sometimes the kidney. Always one of those internal organs. And still, stomach, guts, or (pedantically) intestinal fortitude. Also, lower down, balls, stones, rocks. *Cojones.* Bottle. Bottom. Sand. Always the same unasked, and so unanswered, question: Do you have it? Do you have *them*?

It might seem surprising that style in the sense of fashion should meet style in the form of grace-under-pressure on the unlikely field of the lakeside cabin or trout-filled stream. You might not expect to hear disputes over niceties of attire mixing with talk of violence, Cary Grant mixed in with Ernest Hemingway as role models. Certainly there are those, from ex-girlfriends to perfect strangers, who have *openly doubted* that I was really capable of landing a fish— presumably based on my observed fondness for Italian suits and cocktail bars. A man I did not know even came up to me at a party and said, firmly, *You don't fish*. Not, *I can't believe you fish* or *Do you really fish?* Just, *You don't fish*. I was wearing an Italian suit at the time and drinking a cocktail and so there was, apparently, no room in his conceptual universe for the conjunction.

But there is, after all, a deep link in the overwhelming male desire *to do things well*. Out on the lake or stream, we are trying to display competence and resourcefulness, to organize and succeed, to withstand adversity. We want to succeed, to achieve; and ideally, we want to do so with style. We hardly know, sometimes, what motivates us, what we are seeking, because while there are plenty of manuals and models, lots of advice and warnings, none of them is expansive enough to teach what can be learned only in the doing. We are in pursuit of something large and complex, something at which we both co-operate and compete—a feature of our character that frequently baffles our wives and girl-friends. And, naturally, ourselves.

We are, in short, trying to be men.

And we're going to need equipment to do it.

So much of fishing is concerned with gear that outsiders may be forgiven for thinking it is merely an exercise in technological supremacy, like golf or skiing as they are too often practised, usually at the cost of a healthy bank account and, sometimes, marriage. Certainly it is possible in angling to surrender one's soul to an especially virulent form of the *materiel mania* that afflicts all men now and then. One lesson in fly casting, a birthday gift from a mischievous friend, and my buddy Todd had loaded himself down with hundreds of dollars' worth of rod, reel, line, and flies. Happens in five minutes, sometimes less, and you can understand why: the seductive whip-action of carbon, the near invisibility of the lines and leaders, the furry brightness of new-tied flies lying in an open leather book, bright brass zipper up the sides. Kid in a candy store doesn't do it justice; kid in a candy store *in heaven* is more like it, with the added refinement that he's a grown-up kid with lots of disposable cash and the store smells not of acid drops and licorice whips but is instead layered with hints of open air, leather, whisky, cigar smoke, and burning wood. Eau de Manhood.

When I was living in New York I used to think all of that outdoorsy stuff was impossibly far away, since the city, while surely consumed by its own forms of *materiel mania,* and even able to support a weird form of angler's obsession in its many wharves and riverside vistas, seemed all too distant from the peculiar charms of the Canadian wilderness. But, in thinking this, I had simply forgotten the complex city–country dynamic, that mixture of tension, celebration, and mutual hostility that has sustained angling since time immemorial. The existence of the city underwrites the pursuit of country air as surely as the existence of the city sustains the censure of sin and depravity emanating from the country. The two need each other to live, to be what they suppose themselves to be: sophistication versus simplicity, and virtue versus vice. The pastoral resuscitation always offset by the glittering possibilities and sense of freedom offered by streets and alleys, bars and theatre. Two kinds of freedom, two scales of value, locked in an eternal embrace, each defining itself by contrast with the other.

The city also represents, for anglers, a concentration of expertise and necessary technology. We cannot proceed to the country until we have visited the urban institution of the tackle shop, the place where, deep inside the concrete canyons of Manhattan or Toronto, we imagine the open spaces of Montana or British Columbia. It was Walton himself who advised fledgling anglers, unable to fashion their own rods and lines, to patronize a certain tackle shop in central London: *"Courteous Reader,"* a note in the 1676 edition advises, "You may be pleas'd to take notice, that at the sign of the Three Trouts in St. *Paul's* church-Yard, on the North side, you may be fitted with all sorts of the best Fishing-Tackle, by *John Margrave.*" The earlier editions had also recommended "either Charles Brandon's (near to the Swan in Golding-Lane); or to Mr. Fletcher's, in the Court which did once belong to Dr. Nowel, the Dean of St. Paul's, that I told you was a good man and a good Fisher; it is hard by the West end of St. Paul's Church."

Purveyors of gear have known ever since that the only location better than right beside a lake is two hundred, or two thousand, miles away from the lake. Indeed, the city tackle shop does a far superior business because it trades exclusively in distant dreams, and while a nearby vendor, like a golf course pro shop, can help you solve immediate problems, trading on imminence and proximity, there is in every angler a secret ambition never to use that lifeline. How much better to gear up completely *before even leaving the city limits,* like a soldier going on campaign, and will the rest to fortune and resourcefulness?

I spent so much time walking around New York rather than writing a book I was supposed to be writing that it was probably inevitable I should eventually stumble upon a tackle shop. Which one day I did, on the wide expanse of 23rd Street on the West Side between Seventh and Eighth avenues: Capitol Fishing Tackle Company, with a guitar shop on one flank and a tailor on the other. Now, 23rd is one of the wide two-way streets that mark off discernible chunks in the northward climb of Manhattan and it pretty much set the upper limit of my New York life, so I was glad to find this mecca there, still theoretically within my neighbourhood, or close enough.

It is just a tackle shop, which is itself a minor relief given how many "sportsman's" outlets in that country, and especially in New York, are really fronts for the dissemination of handguns, with rods on one wall, hunting rifles on another, and Glock 9-millimetres, Streetsweepers, and Mac-10s under glass at the counter. The 23rd Street store is on the same stretch as a vintage clothing store, some comic-book shops, and a tattoo parlour. It is big and airy but crammed full of heavily laden shelves of gear: bewildering, uncommunicative doodads in little plastic bags hanging from metal spikes, things I could neither fathom nor remember ever seeing before. The big stuff, the rods and reels, was behind the long counter on the right-hand side, and sitting there, watching my tentative approach, was The Tackle Guy.

The Tackle Guy is a type we've all met, often in humiliating circumstances. He knows all the things we don't, up to and including the state of our half-formed yearning. He is, by necessity, an accomplished angler himself, otherwise he would not be in charge of dispensing the gear. That is the absolute presupposition we bring to the experience of buying tackle; to question it, even for one moment, would be to undermine the entire logic of gear. And yet he is here, in the city rather than fishing, which raises a scintilla of doubt. But the logic quickly reasserts itself. His presence here somehow manages to suggest not a lack of interest in fishing but a further refinement thereof. Of *course* he's not fishing now! He'll fish for just the three best weeks of the season on a stream you've never heard of, somewhere in a state with lots of vowels, accessible only by float plane and a three-day hike, and if you have the nerve to ask where it is, he'll just laugh.

Like the hosts of those down-home Saturday-morning fishing shows, he talks in a baffling insider lingo, probably in a Southern accent, that wards off the uninitiated as surely as a science-fiction force field. Your best hope with The Tackle Guy is always, *always* that he will simply take pity on you. This is your only play. You cannot talk to him as an equal because you are demonstrably his inferior. You cannot approach him with too much abject need or he will despise you. You must exhibit the fine-tuned combination of want and humility that will mark you as a fellow Brother of the Angle, if still mostly in thought rather than deed.

"How's it going," I said to The Tackle Guy, affecting a casual flatness I didn't feel. *Gear! Gear everywhere!* I looked near rather than at him, scanning the forbidding shelves behind him with a distraction I fancied was mistakable for keen interest.

"Not bad," he said. "What do you need?"

I have no freaking idea, I wailed inwardly. I need to fish and not look stupid doing it. I need to catch lots of fish and impress my brother Sean and his buddy Fred, and make my brother Steve a little green with envy along the way. I need to land a big fat trout so impressive all the other guys will just look at it and laugh in appreciation. I need to tell the story later to my pal Julian, a wizard of English chalkstream fishing, over a Partagas cigar and a martini in some rooftop bar in the dead of city winter and have him nod approvingly. I need . . .

"Um, I'm sort of thinking of buying a fly rod," I said, adding, in a doomed attempt to sound a little more impressive, "I'm going to British Columbia in a couple of weeks to fish for trout."

"Stream or lake?" he said, without looking up from some arcane manual of incomprehensible angling lore. "Wet flies or dry? Stocked lake? If it's a stocked lake, you don't need a rod, you just need your hand. They'll eat corn, those things. Ha ha ha. They'll jump right into the boat, you don't even have to fish, just stand there like an idiot."

He started to laugh harder and I could feel my face going blank. Corn? *Corn?* What's wrong with corn? I almost told him that the great Viscount Grey of Falloden, Foreign Minister of Great Britain, once used corn to land a five-pound trout on the River Test back in the spring of Ought-One. I have no idea if this is true, am pretty sure it is not and maybe couldn't be, but his disdain was bugging me. Never despise corn, you arrogant jerk! Corn is bait! All successful bait is honourable bait! Success is the only argument! Izaak Walton used corn!

I'm not quite sure that is true either, but The Tackle Guy must have sensed my mounting if ill-informed pique because his attitude immediately softened and we got down to the happy business of curbing my stupid enthusiasm. The writer John Gierach relates how his first visit to a tackle shop involved questions like "What size fly do I need to catch a twenty-inch brown trout?" and "How do I tie the itsy-bitsy fly onto the big fat line?" (Answer: Well, first you'll need a *leader*.) "A clerk in the average fly shop," Gierach says, "spends half his time patiently leading people from the middle back to somewhere near the beginning." And that's about right. Of course, he spends the other half making fun of those people by joshing around with his more accomplished customers.

No, that's not true. A good Tackle Guy knows your weaknesses but doesn't exploit them, if only because it would be unsporting to do so and he is used to having the very same thought on the stream or lake. My Tackle Guy, who turned out to be ex-Marine with claims of fearsome combat in Korea and good fishing most other places in the world, was a pretty good guy. He understood implicitly the need we all have to succeed instantly, and why that simply can't happen. He showed me a rod or two, critiqued my casting motion, and recommended some flies. I left without buying anything, and I could not decide later whether this had been my choice or his.

Only some time after, while reading Arthur Ransome, did I realize that I had experienced what Ransome calls the *Platonic tackle-shop visit*. Our weakness as anglers, amateur and expert alike, says Ransome, must be met by the gentle restraint of the good tackle-shop owner, who will recognize a Platonic seeker and put away the superlative rod rather than let the customer spend his money. Otherwise he risks losing a regular client, since, as Ransome remarks, "to have to carry through the streets a brand-new rod as proof that you have needed comfort on account of an inability to go fishing is a searing experience, not to be easily forgotten." Bad tackle-dealers will lose a customer by pressing their business, and this is unwise for "no man likes to revisit the scene of a public loss of self-control." My Tackle Guy had flirted but not consummated; he'd thrown me back, knowing I would all too probably bite again when I was a little bigger.

Not every Tackle Guy can be counted on for this display of forbearance, of course, and we have to learn to be somewhat self-regulating. This is not easy. Like all gear-related undertakings, angling takes on an acquisitive life of its own. We want to fish, and we want to fish better. The lure of stuff is the promise of improvement: graphite rods, precision-bearing reels, vanishing leads, and killer flies. There is also, somewhere in there, once again, a version of Veblen's principle of ostentatious consumption: the guy with the best gear may not be the best angler, but he has the most money and time to devote to our passion and, in this alone, evinces a certain superiority. The gentleman of leisure, Veblen writes in *The Theory of the Leisure Class,* "becomes a connoisseur in creditable viands of various degrees of merit, in manly beverages and trinkets, in seemly apparel and architecture, in weapons, games, dances, and narcotics. This cultivation of the aesthetic faculty requires time and application, and the demands made upon the gentleman in this direction therefore tend to change his life of leisure into a more or less arduous application to the business of learning how to live a life of ostensible leisure in a becoming way."

Of course, most of the time it's far simpler: we just want to look cool. John Gierach describes the feelings of sick envy, surely widespread, occasioned by other, better-equipped anglers. "The stuff fly-fishermen carried was both beautiful and serious looking at the same time—like a big, jangling ring of keys to a different reality." The other guys on the river looked, Gierach says, like "combinations of tackle stores, biology labs, and hospital emergency wards." He concludes that he *needs more stuff,* not just a rod and reel and flies, but "enough stuff to make me clank and rattle when I walked." This desire to look cool, like almost all others, has costs both obvious and unforeseen. Soon the angler is helpless, in the grip of a powerful *voidophobia:* "the unreasonable fear of empty vest pockets." There are more and more trips to the tackle shop. The Tackle Guy becomes his best, maybe only, friend, and he disappears from everyday life for longer and longer periods. Not long after that, his marriage breaks up over a series of financial disputes.

Who Is Fred?

It's never entirely about the gear. The gear is only a means to an end. But the gear is seductive. It has a life of its own. It must be approached with caution.

"I need some wet flies for trout," I told The Tackle Guy in New York on my next, inevitable visit a week later. This was just before my second Weekend of fishing, when I was obviously hooked.

"No problem," he said, and pulled from beneath the counter an intimidating tray of flies all sorted into little plastic compartments. "They are all good for trout. They have different hackles and details." The names were half familiar: Dun, Coachman, Dr. Cahill. Working more from aesthetics than knowledge, I started picking out flies from the boxes and placing them on the counter. Only after I had piled up four or five did I realize that they might be different prices, and now I wouldn't be able to say which was which. They all looked indistinguishably grey. I realized I was not entirely sure what part of the fly was the hackle. My hand froze over the big tray.

"Are these all the same price?"

"Sure." He was not even looking at me.

I finished making my little pile of exquisite tiny insectoid hooks, wondering if any of them would work out in British Columbia or on the rivers in southern Ontario. The Guy flicked them neatly into a little plastic case and took my money.

"Good luck," he said to my back as I walked out onto spring-bright 23rd Street. I didn't turn or look around. I said nothing. I simply raised a hand in salute and kept on walking.

Just for the record, every one of those five flies, picked more for looks than anything more rational, worked like a charm out on the lake in the Okanagan Valley, hooking more than a dozen fish in an afternoon. One of them, a tiny speckled grey, landed a thirteen-and-a-half-inch wild rainbow, the biggest fish of the weekend, and won me a couple of cigars from Sean and Fred. It caught my eye; then it caught the fish's—and what could be better than that?

Fred impresses me for many reasons, not least that he has the jangling, laden vest of the experienced angler. And watching Fred tie flies in the cabin, his clamp set on the table after the dinner dishes have been cleared away, is mesmerizing and humbling. Tiny barbless hooks, hardly more than twists of wire; silk thread and pheasant feather; hackles and wings and beads; the subtle details of colour and size and shape. All minutely detailed to mimic a mayfly larva or full-grown mosquito or midge. Fred swirls and winds the thread, adds a feather, takes a feather away, and finishes the microscopic masterpiece with a practised flourish of knotting. A perfect green nymph ready for the leader. I think: I'll never be able to do that—that little flick and pinch with the tying key that rounds off the threading and makes the fly whole.

Flies themselves are lovely things, useful but beautiful in their purpose, gorgeous when displayed in leather books or under glass cases, the multi-hued machinery of death. Most of them have traditional names that, especially in the English lexicon, mention their entomological origins or distinctive silhouettes: Hare's Ears, the Lead-Winged Coachman, Olive Quill, Iron-Blue Dun, Dotterel Dun, Honey-Dun Hen Hackle, the Blue Hawk. Sometimes, as with the Dr. Cahill or Tupp's Indispensable, they allude, not very clearly, to some early practitioner of the art of fly-tying. Just as the British, in contrast to their more overt North American cousins, tend to favour ironic or genteel names for other violent machines—who else, for example, would call a fighter plane a Pup, a Camel, or a Dart?—so their fly names remain archaic and Waltonian. American innovations, by contrast, tend to bear names like Terminator and Slayer, which somehow seem to violate the genteel spirit of fly fishing, whatever the similar outcome of a landed trout. Or is it maybe American straightforwardness over English hypocrisy?

Anyway, the language of flies exhibits the same combination of elegance and ferocity that underwrites the sport more generally, not to mention that pleasing cadence of expertise casually deployed. G.E.M. Skues, for example, compares two similar flies in a passage of swooning impenetrability from his classic *The Way of a Trout with a Fly* (1924): "Each has a peacock herl body. The dun of the starling wings in the Coachman is reproduced by the dun centre of the hackle of the Little Chap, and the red hackle of the Coachman by the red points of the hackle of the Little Chap. But if they be dressed on the same size of hook, when one will kill, as a general proposition the other will kill." To which the only reasonable duffer's response is, *I believe you.*

Despite his many virtues, Fred's presence on the fishing Weekends violated the implicit Kingwells-only policy, not to mention complicating our two-men-to-a-boat logistics. But this turned out to be good news for everybody, and not just because his grilled prawns and pesto linguine went down so well after a day on the lake. He also had the outsider's ability to put moronic family conflicts into context, so that the nightly games of Hearts—that meanest of childish card games—did not degenerate into the shouting matches and semi-serious shoving that might otherwise have come from the combination of four hyper-competitive Kingwells and a little too much wine over dinner. These cheery card games always threaten to become all too reminiscent of the ugly Trivial Pursuit free-for-alls of the 1980s or the hockey-watching debacles of the early 1990s. Nobody really wanted a repeat of these scenes; they make it hard to go out fishing together the next day.

Growing up with two brothers, each of us separated by five years, there was always a fair amount of blood from routine boyhood violence. We all have the fine network of scar tissue on our hands and knees and elbows from cuts and slashes and jabs that are a part of a life's ascent into manhood. There were also a couple of spectacular injuries. The summer I was nine, a recoiling air-rifle handle caught me in the right eye and sliced open my eyelid—one of those small cuts that releases a terrifying stream of blood, which seeped through my fingers and down my face. I remember running home, and then sitting next to my mother in her car while she, cigarette in her mouth and panic in her heart because she thought I'd lost an eye, frantically drove me to the hospital on the air force base where we lived. One stitch on the eyelid was enough, but neither of us had known that during the worst car ride of my life, me with a blood-soaked tea towel pressed to my eye.

And there was the time Sean, in another military house in another part of the country, en route from the downstairs fridge where the soft drinks were stored, slipped on some water I had spilled on the basement floor. He was about eleven. Falling, he hit the exposed concrete with the bottle still cradled in his left arm, smashing it and driving a big knife-like wedge of glass deep into his forearm. Upstairs I heard the crash and said to myself, in my best Howard Cosell interior voice, *Down goes Kingwell! Down goes Kingwell!* Then I heard the panicked yelling. His gash is still the nastiest and most shocking laceration I have seen up close; it went bone-deep across the diagonal width of his arm. And every time I see the snake of untannable scars on his arm—the cut itself plus long surgical incisions to repair nerve damage—I think of that open mouth of dark red muscle on the white flesh, the fear in his eyes as he came running up the basement steps.

I got hit by a car the day I graduated high school, riding my bike down Wellington Crescent in Winnipeg, and that was a nasty spill, all right, with long cuts from the car's grille down my left calf and across my right knee, and a layer of skin torn off most of my right thigh where the loose bike shorts I was wearing rode up, my leg scraping across asphalt as I slid to a stop in the middle of the road. The impact almost, but not quite, broke my left leg; instead the leg swelled up to twice its normal size, sporting a gruesome purple contusion that faded and kaleidoscoped to various greens and yellows over the next few weeks of couch-riding convalescence. That was bad, and stupid, too, since I wasn't wearing a helmet, but it didn't really *hurt* except for a dismal half-hour lying on an emergency room gurney as the shock wore off and it felt like someone was carefully plying the length of my leg with hot knives.

The injury I remember most, however, was the time Steve, that shameless goon, the Kim Clackson of the sandlot and backyard, broke my arm. He denies this, of course, but the facts are pretty clear. Under the crude basketball hoop we had bolted above the garage door at the house in Winnipeg, playing lazy one-on-one on the wet tarmac, he fouled me so hard on an outside jumpshot that I came down with my ass well back of my feet. I fell backwards and instinctively stuck out my arms to break the fall, in the process hyperextending and jamming the fibula of my left one. A green-stick fracture, when the bone doesn't actually break but sort of buckles and twists in the middle like a young branch. It hurt like hell, though, a low throb that built slowly over the next hour to unignorable pain. Steve laughed when I told him I wanted to go to the hospital. Come to that, he laughed when I fell, too. I had to call our father at work and ask him to come home and take me to the emergency room.

This kind of overt violence—yes, yes, I know, he denies the whole thing—was fairly unusual for Steve, who was more often an accomplished but subtle rec room terrorist and after-school bully. In our daily battles over TV channel control, toy appropriation, and basement space, especially as I grew bigger and almost as tall as him, Steve quickly adopted an expansionist foreign policy, backed up with big stick military intervention. He was expert in the principle of delayed retaliation. Bracing myself for the return shot during one of our frequent tussles, I would see Steve's face suddenly relax into a wintry smile. "Don't worry, Mark," he would say, "I'm not going to hit you *now*. But I *will* get you back, sometime before you go to bed tonight. You won't know when it's coming. But before bed."

Nerves on edge like a hunted animal, I cringed and cowered at his merest feint in my direction as evening slowly became night. Steve was adept at the delays, too—a crucial refinement. Sometimes he would wait until my guard was entirely down, when I was brushing my teeth or saying good night to our parents, and then he would dance in, Ali-style, from the other room and clip me smartly across the back of the head, then juke gleefully out of the way when I tried to hit back. I credit this experience for my later deep understanding of the principle of nuclear deterrence.

Sitting in the boat one morning at the lake, it occurred to me that, all other issues aside, I owe Steve a broken arm.

"You won't know when it's coming, Steve," I whispered softly to myself, slowly hauling line on my last cast. "But sometime soon. Sometime before you die." I pulled the line a few more feet and gave vent to a low cackle of cinematic evil-mastermind laughter. "Talk? No, Mr. Bond. I expect you to *die*."

So, anyway, all in all it was good that Fred was there, a placid presence capable of ensuring minimal civil behaviour. But even more than these considerable contributions, Fred fulfilled the ancient and honourable role of *gillie,* the expert semi-outsider whose stores of lake wisdom and common sense make the rest of us look good. Sean, to be sure, has no need of this, being just as accomplished an angler. But Sean is our younger brother, which means that Steve and I cannot possibly listen to him. Fred is the perfect guide, combining a regimental sergeant-major's desire for competence with the Zen-like placidity of a pitching coach.

Like all good anglers, Fred also illustrates the ancient aesthetic maxim that the exercise of skill is an end in itself. Which sounds complicated but isn't. On the other hand, it is *deep,* and in the way sometimes only simple things can be. Which means maybe it's time for a new chapter.

But before that, a story—in the form of a letter from my father. It doesn't illustrate *sprezzatura,* exactly, but it does say something about style:

Catch & Release

Hi Mark:

*After we were talking I remembered a story. I don't
know if you recall, but one time you, Steven, and I
drove from Toronto to Quebec to see my parents. I think
we were still in Clinton, so you were pretty young. My
grandfather's house in the country had been closed up
for a while then, but my mother got it opened up so we
could spend some time there. There was a little brook
that ran through my uncle's place adjacent to my grandfather's and it had (and had had since I was a boy) a
nice supply of speckled trout. They came up the brook
from Rivière aux Pins, which also ran through my
uncle's property in the spring when the water was high,
and then got trapped in the pools when the water went
down. They had plenty of food and so grew quite nicely.*

*I had fished for them when I was a boy, with fishing
line tied to a pole cut from the alder bushes, where you
shortened your line as required by winding it around
the pole, small fish hooks, and fat juicy worms. I wish
I could remember how old Steve was, but anyway old
enough to want to try his hand. The way I remember
him is sitting on the brook bank, with infinite patience
dangling his worm in the water while the mosquitoes,
which were absolutely awful that summer, tried to eat
him alive. Of course, there was no reel on the pole, nor*

Who Is Fred?

indeed any room, what with the overhanging bushes, to
"play" a fish anyway, so if you got a bite, you just tried
to yank the fish out of the water.

I remember Steve got a bite and yanked so hard that
the fish flew off the hook and up over the telephone
lines and landed in the dirt road behind us. Still
another kind of fishing, I guess you could say.

Love, Dad

I'm sorry to have to report that Steve, though undeniably stylish in other respects, not least his complement of Brooks Brothers suits, has advanced his angling technique only marginally since then. He still has a tendency to slap his backcast on the water behind him. He still tries to horse his fish right out of the water when he's got a bite, dragging a tiny rainbow trout bouncing across the surface of the lake. And if he thinks he has a strike, which is rather more often than evidence and rational judgement would allow, he has perfected a wild attempted hook-set that sends his fly up and out of the water, sailing over our ducking heads.

On the other hand, he has yet to hurl a trout all the way into the dirt. And I suppose you might call that progress.

5

The Exercise of Skill Is an End in Itself

"Next to being an expert, it is well to be a contented duffer: a man who would fish if he could, and who will please himself by flicking off his flies, and dreaming of impossible trout, and smoking among the sedges Hope's enchanted cigarettes. Next time we shall be more skilled, more fortunate. Next time!"

—Andrew Lang, *Angling Sketches*

*S*ean, clearly thinking like the military tactician he might have been, had distributed an exhaustive list of supplies the urbanites—which is to say, Steve and myself, coming at this point from New York and Boston—would have to bring along for the very first Weekend. This list included such predictable items as warm clothes and rain gear, a hat, and (my favourite) "shoes you don't care about." I think it may fairly be said that these are something even the most elegant man must have in his wardrobe, and in my case they were a shapeless old pair of slate-blue Pumas with the heels worn down. Nope, don't care about those.

I think it's also fair to say that the only times a grown man may acceptably wear a baseball cap, if he is white and middle-class, anyway, is while (a) jogging in the rain, (b) actually playing baseball, or (c) off somewhere fishing. Dress-code purists, liable to get upset when men stroll into a high-end downtown eatery wearing a shirt and tie *but no jacket,* or with some sort of sweater pulled over, or with anything other than belt and shoes fashioned of leather, could wish that the baseball-cap rule were more widely observed. What is it with North American men and baseball caps, anyway? What are they hoping to accomplish? Trying to remain young, sporty, athletic? Attempting to look cool in the eyes of their peers, sons, prospective girlfriends? Whatever the reasons, there they are, in bars and on the street, walking downtown and driving in their cars, the men being boys—or something—by sporting the cap. Clearly a project doomed to failure.

I brought a ball cap for the fishing trip, an old beige number with a leather strap in back and, get this, absolutely no logo or message of any kind in front. You would be surprised—well, no, of course you *wouldn't*— how hard it is to find a baseball cap in this world that displays neither writing nor symbol, no claims of forgotten golf tournaments, manufacturer's corporate signage, or stylized sports-team letters. It's an achievement and I have treasured this cap for some time, to the extent, actually, that it was misshapen and sweat-stained beyond all propriety, deeply furrowed, and coloured by sun and dirt from dark brown to bleach white. When we were caught in heavy rain, the cap soaked and then leaked impressively discoloured drops of sweaty moisture from the half-crushed bill. I also had my meagre supply of foul-weather gear, a hooded shell and an insulated waterproof jacket I bought one winter in Cambridge.

What I hadn't brought was something I hadn't even thought to remember: earplugs. Sean, the gearmeister, produced these with a flourish as we were divvying up rooms for the night. The cabin was a comfortable venue, with lots of room for all, but it did involve me sharing a room with Steve, a notorious snorer, Dad taking the little fold-out bed in the main room, Sean and Fred upstairs in the little loft under the wooden eaves. We each took a pair of the spongy pink plugs and jammed them in our ears.

My bedding had been supplied by Dad, who had packed it into his truck before leaving Vancouver Island to join Sean and Fred in their little convoy into the interior. It was a rolled blanket fixed by an old bungee cord I remembered from the back of my father's Honda motorcycle, a smart dark green 500cc model that dated from his second, GWG-Road-Kings-jean-jacket mid-life crisis, circa 1977. (Not to be confused with his first, moustache-sporting, Ford-Torino mid-life crisis of 1973.) The blanket was a worn grey square of raspy wool edged with thin blue lines and decorated with the badges and neckerchiefs I had earned as a Cub and Scout.

There they were, the little gold-backed red and blue stars, the rounded triangles of merit badges with their tiny threaded images of a fire, a compass, a vacuum cleaner. Yes, housekeeping: my easiest merit badge. I was transported instantly to the church basements and rec halls of air force bases in Summerside and Winnipeg where I'd worn them, the ritual greetings and quasi-military boxing matches and winter orienteering ventures of the whole sick Baden-Powell moral-hygiene universe, which I'm sorry to say bore little resemblance to the jaunty Cavalier military dandyism I'd hoped for.

I suddenly pictured Scouter Russ and Scouter Stu, the two ramrod-straight ex-army wack-jobs who used to run the thin, dispirited scouting group at CFB Winnipeg in the mid-1970s. One of them, Russ or Stu, boasted a luxuriant RAF-style moustache and mad glinting eyes; the other, Stu or Russ, was tall, thin, and sadistic. They both wore regimental flashes, knotted lanyards attached to drill whistles, and the rainbow-hued ribbons of massed infantry decorations on their dark green button-pocketed scouting shirts. Russ (maybe Stu) was English, or pretended to be, and spoke in the sort of accent I had only ever heard in a Derek-and-Clive comedy sketch mocking the bloodthirsty insanity of a retired colonel in the proverbial *Imagine-this-mustard-pot-is-the-Fifth-Punjabi-Rifles* mode. They both made us box and do push-ups and chin-ups and other exercises intended to build muscle and character. Also burpees, which I think were invented by the Canadian military for the express purpose of making recruits look stupid. They involve spastic squats combined with a violent backward fling of the legs, then a smart return to the upright position. Imagine a combined vertical/horizontal piston composed of a human body pumping away, twenty to the minute. *Fifty more burpees, guys! C'mon, guys! Builds character!*

Catch & Release

In those days a battalion of the Princess Patricia's Canadian Light Infantry, a dozen of whose members were later killed or wounded by friendly U.S. Air National Guard fire in Afghanistan, was stationed in Winnipeg. The PPCLIs, an elite airborne regiment, were notorious for being the most gung-ho outfit in the Canadian army, a reputation they took very, very seriously. I don't know if Russ and Stu had actually served with the Princess Pats but they sure as hell wanted us to think they had. They were the kind of Scout leaders who taught you to abseil backwards down a rock face by kicking your feet and pushing you over the edge. *Go, you maggot! Move your feet! Builds character!* I felt my arms give a sympathetic twinge at the memory of a thousand long-ago push-ups and burpees.

My father had another surprise for me. He produced a cookie tin lined with waxed paper and held it open. Inside, the crescent moons and twisted pastry packages of my favourite homemade biscuits, the nutty sugar-dusted kipferl of my childhood, passed down from my Austrian grandmother to my mother, feature of so many Christmases past. I took a couple. They say music is the most evocative of memories, and indeed, its uncanny ability to transport one is perhaps the closest thing to time travel we know. But really, food, with its unbeatable combination of taste and smell, is the vastly more satisfying medium. Kipferl are my madeleines.

I went to sleep happy. Until, that is, Steve's snoring—snoring to rival a fairy-tale giant's, snoring of titanic dimension, cutting-edge earplugs notwithstanding—woke me and kept me awake. "Negligible at first, and almost amusing," says a character in Louis Begley's *About Schmidt*, "like the whirring of a hobbyist's model airplane or the buzz of a mad fly, one doesn't mind it because it will end very soon, as soon as the toy engine runs down. Instead, the noise gathers strength, turns fearsomely rowdy and urgent, vastly larger than the placid, self-satisfied body from which it issues, and only a stake driven through the sleeper's heart will make it stop."

About three a.m., exhausted and full of the usual nagging worries of the habitual insomniac now supplemented by thoughts of how I was going to manage dumping Steve's lifeless body into the lake before dawn, I fell into a second, fitful sleep.

We rose early the next morning, eager to get onto the water even though May trout sometimes don't rouse themselves to feed until mid-morning. Steve and I were still on Eastern time and so our circadian clocks popped us into consciousness well before seven a.m. Dad was in charge of breakfast, which could have been disastrous since he is a fussy cook, liable to use every available utensil in even the most advanced kitchen in order to secure the toasting of bread or boiling of water. He is not quite the Bad Camp Cook of trout-fishing lore, the sort who, as John Gierach says, "mix cans of spaghetti and chili together in the same pan as a way of continuing to punish their mothers for something." But it can be a near thing. Anyway, Dad was in good form that morning, puttering and muttering efficiently enough over the sausages and fried eggs, while I made toast by holding pieces of white bread over the open gas flame with a fork. He also hauled out an old glass-topped tin percolator that I remembered burbling on the battered green-and-red Coleman stove of numerous family camping trips along the north shore of Lake Superior and in the Rocky Mountain foothills. It popped, hissed, and groaned as if in great pain and dispensed a dense, heavily caffeinated sludge that is to regular coffee as, I suppose, crack cocaine is to barley sugar.

Bright-eyed and caparisoned for battle, loaded with rods and reels and line, we hopped into the two boats and putt-putted out to the farthest corner of the lake, the boats loaded with all the necessary extra supplies including boat-beers and granola bars. Every angler knows that, thus provisioned, he can stay out fishing indefinitely. It is also widely known that boat-beer, unlike regular beer, has a refreshing rather than intoxicating effect. That is why it can be consumed *at any time during the day* with no untoward result. In fact, boat-beer is well known to tone you up and improve both coordination and judgement. Certain conditions must of course be met, including (a) the boat-beer must be consumed while one is actually in the boat, (b) the boat must be out upon the water, not merely moored somewhere, and (c) the boat-beer should, for preference, be Kokanee, a brand widely celebrated in the Western regions of this country for containing absolutely no alcohol.

The sun was shining and it was warm enough for us to want to shed our shirts. I found that my cargo pants, loaded with PowerBars, were falling off my hips. I tightened my belt and thought, not for the first time that spring, that I wasn't eating enough. New York was making me skinny. Maybe it was all the walking I was doing, or the fact that my then-girlfriend lived in a six-floor walk-up where every visit and grocery trip was a StairMaster workout. But maybe it was the sheer force of osmotic anxiety. The throb of the city around me was actually melting the ounces from my middle, like a spiritual sauna. For the first time since I'd left Manhattan for the airport twenty-four hours before, I felt the utter difference between there and here.

It wasn't the noise level, really, though that was part of it. We speak of the silence of the river or lake, but the truth is that, even without car horns and air brakes and the near-constant wail of sirening EMS vehicles stuck in traffic, there is plenty of sound around us: the buzzing of flies, wind sighing through the shoreline pine stands, trout jumping and plopping back in the inky, cold water. But the *density* is entirely different. There is no trace of the warm crushing weight that is New York's daily charm and burden—the swirling gravitational force of eight million other souls all packed into a few dozen square miles and there seeking, always seeking, something like happiness, or merely survival. Here, on the lake, there were just four of us, countless trout we wanted to catch, and the wide open, blue British Columbia sky. The air was so big and pure that for a moment I felt dizzy, the way you do when you finally venture outside into winter cold when you've been laid up for a week with the flu. Like the first hit of a drug.

I started to believe that, maybe, fishing wasn't so stupid after all.

Fred handed me a loaded rod, a small wet-fly nymph on the end of the leader, and said, "Okay, Mark, I know you don't really want to. But try a cast."

Fishing for trout with flies, wet or dry, is all about the cast. Everybody knows this. But, like playing shortstop or tying a bow tie, casting is also more complicated and exacting than you think if you've never done it. The movement of loading up the line feels natural, deceptively so, as when you wind up to throw a baseball, say, or swing an axe: ancient muscle memory, the family of swinging, throwing motions we must surely get from our distant hominid ancestors. And the grace of the unspooling line when it goes well is one of the purest physical pleasures you can imagine. It's the deep satisfaction of something old and well thought-out, a human skill practised with little variation for centuries. But it is, for all the same reasons, supremely difficult to master.

With dry flies the task is even harder because you're trying to lay the airy little bundle of feather and silk right on the surface of the water, unwinding the coiled line with a long rolling motion that gently deposits your hidden hook right where a submerged trout will think it is one more alighting insect. It's true that dry-fly rigging is less cumbersome than a nymph set-up, with its long leaders and tiny Styrofoam strike indicator, but this is more than offset by the lightness of the pure dry fly, which makes accurate long casting a daunting challenge. You want the fly to land as far as possible away from you, your sloshing legs, and your dangerous shadow. Your line is hollow plastic, light enough to stay on the surface of the water, with a filament of all but invisible lead on the end, where you want the fish to see only fly, not line.

The subtle balance of dry-fly fishing lies fundamentally in the trade-offs of hook and weight. A dry-fly hook can be little more than a tiny bend of wire, no bigger than a stud earring, that will sail through the air and hit the water surface with a compelling lightness. However, such a hook—even if you can manage to sling it accurately through the air, make it look convincingly appetizing, and set it in the gulping rainbow's sharp mouth—will almost certainly work itself loose if the fish decides to fight. And he will.

Once you have laid down your dry fly, waiting for a strike takes patience and guile. Depending on the conditions, you may want to cast just upstream of the likely hideout, which is, say, a stump or rock cluster in the middle of a decent brook flow, with good feeding front and back and enough calm down below to make an attractive home. The fly must be of the sort the fish is taking that day—that hour of the day—since, especially in good feeding areas where the trout are worth catching, they are also picky eaters. Changing your fly after five or ten unsuccessful casts is by no means excessive or impatient. In May, by every classical account the best month for trout, you might find yourself offering green in the morning, that delightful period before the day gets too hot, then switching to brown or black in the late afternoon. And not just colour. You might use Coachmen and Chaps and numerous other combinations of artificial wing and body.

You have to wait until the fly is inside the trout's mouth or you will set it too lightly in the lip. Or you will miss the set altogether. Trout, like all fish in their class, don't really bite; they suck water through their mouth and gills, and swallow. Ideally, you want to set your hook as the trout has the entire fly inside its mouth, preferably on the tough inside of the mouth. Waiting for the right moment to snap the rod, when the trout is breaking the surface or sucking the fly down, is an exercise in judgement and composure, especially after waiting long minutes and maybe hours to get a strike—enough to defeat all but the most equable of men. Thus is mere fishing made the art of the angle.

Wet-fly fishing is easier, so much so that true purists are apt to disdain it, creating the usual sort of ultra-fine distinction within distinction by which all human activities, especially the useless leisure ones, are marked. Grey, who does not disdain wet flies, nevertheless begins one of his chapters with customary modesty, which incidentally illustrates the issue. "It is with much diffidence that any attempt can be made to describe the delights of dry fly fishing," he says.

"Those who know and practise the art best are the epicures among anglers; they have carried both the skill and the pleasure of angling to a height of exquisite refinement, and to them I fear that any detailed account of a day's dry fly fishing must seem inadequate." Very possibly, but Grey directs himself instead to the "very large majority" that are not so blessed, and thank God for that. We can't all be epicures; at least, we can't all start out that way, for then, where would we go in search of further refinements of our sport? What would we have to aim for?

The line and leader for wet flies are similar to those for dry, often identical. But they can be heavier, and therefore easier to cast, because your creative deception this time involves less subtle placement of the fly. It can plop into the water with a certain clumsy energy and still do its work in attracting fish. Your aim is to imitate not the surface-dipping airborne insect but the submerged larval stage of the insect, say a mayfly, as it moves from its underwater eggs to transformation on the beckoning surface. Wet flies can be either mid or lower depth, depending on which stage of the insect's life you are attempting to mimic. Dry flies are imitations of the insect's wing-spreading transformation on the surface; wet flies can be depictions of either the sub-surface fly, with tiny wings, or the larval stage found lower down. Wet flies are often better when angling for smaller trout in mountain lakes, where schools of them feed below the surface of certain corners and pools.

Since I haven't, and won't, share with you the name of the British Columbia lake where the Weekends take place, I can instead tell you that Sean and Fred were getting strike after strike with wet flies, more specifically nymph or lower depth flies, imitating green chironomids on leaders about five feet long. So was I, once I mastered the rudiments of the cast. And good luck to you.

Setting the hook of a wet fly is a different prospect from the subtle eye–hand undertaking of concentrating on a surface-borne dry fly. Because the fly falls below the surface on a heavier-than-water leader, you can't see it. Nor can you see the rise of the fish to the presented fly. So you must depend on the action of a tiny foam float marked with colour, usually DayGlo red or orange. Or you can, if you've got good touch, hold the rod loosely in your fingers and just wait for the tiny pull on the line that indicates a hit below the surface.

Which, as so often, sounds simple. But the float, a little piece of technology expensive beyond all reason, can be extremely hard to see on the sun-dappled surface of the lapping lake. And even when it's in plain view, concentrating your gaze for long, agonizing minutes is harder and more testing than you'd imagine. It keeps bobbing out of view, indistinguishable from the light-flecked ripples of the water, the bubbles of coursing current or random disturbance. Feeling the tug of a small trout strike requires the manual sensitivity of a concert pianist. You are straining, straining, looking and looking, but trying, all the while, to stay completely relaxed.

And now you see, maybe for the first time, the difference between concentrating and thinking. Fishing is reflective because it empties the mind of the task-oriented cares of everyday life, makes room for thought. But much of that happens, as it were, at the margins. Fishing isn't like strolling in the woods. It requires your close and undivided attention, and so clears a space of almost timeless emptiness. You fall into the moment and hours pass without any awareness beyond the parting clouds, the rising breeze, a loon's call. But you can't fall entirely into reverie or you will fail. You must make your reflection active, your repose eager. Like playing the field in baseball, still more in cricket, angling will not work unless you match leisure with close attention, a readiness to react swiftly and elegantly when the conditions suddenly demand it.

When the marker bobs, a trout is hitting your delicious fly five feet under the water's surface—or it *might* be, since the marker can bob for all kinds of reasons. If you try to set the hook, you might have success and snap the hook into the trout's mouth or you might just scare away all the fish for yards around. You might, more gruesomely, set your hook by accident deep in the fleeing trout's cheek or eye, and so, after hauling him in by main force, feel a sick bile of disappointment and disgust rise to your throat.

Fishing is not really about fish, in the end—or even the beginning. It's about what we allow ourselves to think, what we see reflected back when we look in the mirror of nature. And one of those things is that, without fairness, there is no contest, and so no victory, only more toxic kinds of defeat.

Whether your fly is dry or wet, a successfully hooked trout will haul out your line, sometimes in an explosive run where your hardest job will be giving him enough line fast enough. If you don't pay out the line quickly, the hook will snap loose. Everybody knows this too.

And thus another finely balanced undertaking, poised on the delicate fulcrum between patience and desire. You want to bring the fish into netting range. He doesn't want to come. You must tire him out. But to do that you have to first let him go, leaning on faith and technique that you will eventually get him back. Let the line go slack, but not so slack that the hook simply works itself out of the mouth.

Keep it tight, in other words, but not so tight that you're just dragging the damn thing or risking a break. Slack but tight, loose but solid. All by feel on the little wand of carbon that is now, with your tiny hook and your filament of line, the only means of bringing an angry three-pound slab of fish muscle into the deadly world of air.

And I say "three-pound" as if I've actually ever caught a trout that big. Dispute continues over the size and weight of the one and only brown trout I have so far landed, but conservative estimate puts it at two-and-a-half, and a glass or two of wine might be sufficient to raise it to the nice round number of three pounds. See the cover of the book to judge for yourself. Be charitable. And if you can't be charitable, have a glass or two of wine and try again.

You let line out, you haul it in. Or you let the reel run the line out, trusting its tension control has been properly set for the size of fish you happen to have. The left hand does all the work now, slowly pulling line between the gripped forefingers of your aching right hand, clamped tight on the rod, bending in a tense beautiful bow. Slowly, slowly, bring in more line. A fly rod doesn't need to work by the action of a reel, like a lure rod or, still more, the main-force action of those big brass winders on deep-sea riggers. Sometimes, especially if you're a semi-hacker like me, the fly reel is little more than a convenient way to keep line out of your way as your fingers do the work. I don't recommend this, just state it as a slightly embarrassing fact. And so, gently—well, gently *but firmly*—you pull more and more of the outcast line back into your domain, working the fish closer and letting him go, working in and paying out, always inexorably shortening the thread-thin tether.

The trout may rest, or appear to rest, only to shoot off with a last desperate burst of speed. He may try this last desperate burst a few times, because that's the kind of demon he is. He may dive down, or run for the safety of weeds and submerged trees, where your line will tangle or break, or your hook come free, mangled beyond further use. He may make a dash for the boat or where you are standing, killing all tension in the line and so loosening the hook. You can't see any of this, you can only feel it, and you must react.

And then, finally, when your right arm is sore and tensed as if you have been challenged to a one-armed push-up contest, your wrist set to break, when your back and legs ache with the effort of concentrated attention while standing in the fast current of the river or rocking boat, you will have him close enough to grab or net, tired and still angry, angry and still hooked, and you will be able, if you are calm—though your heart is beating fast—to bend and, holding the meagre essential line still tight, always tight, slip a net or hand under his fat body and lift him, exhausted and yours, into the killing oxygen.

But first, the cast. Always the cast. Like so many others before me, it was while casting that I fell in love with fly fishing. A good cast is its own argument; it is entirely self-justifying. All the rest is bonus.

You haul back and wait for the airy line to weave its looping path, adding more length with every pull, spinning yards of filament in the air above and behind you, looking to the overhung pool or rippled cove where the fish are jumping for food. And there it is: that sublime, dispute-ending conjunction of utility and beauty, the opportunity to offer little grace notes with a flick of the rod, the familiar movements as you come forward and let the shot go. This is so wonderful that you want to do it over and over again, always, like throwing a football or playing catch until your arm goes numb. It is as if the coding is inscribed somewhere down below the conscious level, past objections and hesitations and bad memories.

Of course, if you think about it too much, you've probably just muffed the cast. The line is dying in a pathetic little tangle five feet ahead of you, or the nearly invisible flyweight leader is tangled around a branch in what looks like a multi-fractal problem in theoretical physics. Sure, you have all the tools and the fish have nothing. But the tools are precise and elegant and must be respected. If you're not careful, they work against you. In common with a base hit or a long putt, casting is difficult enough to make true success an event.

And so the fly-fishing cast is beautiful and satisfying beyond all reason; or rather, forces reason to catch up, to expand its horizon to include the cast. Its intent is of course linked intimately to the larger project of deception in which you are engaged, but somehow it takes on a life of its own, becomes its own universe of effort and achievement. The basic principle, as mentioned, is simple. The longer the cast, the farther from your disturbing human presence the fly can be deposited, a coiled and dangerous artificial intrusion into the natural world of feeding fish, potential death waiting with its hidden hook. The more line you can spin into the air above you, the more yards of singing wet light-catching gossamer you can coax into the hanging pattern of figure eights in front and behind you, the tiny hook waiting as you pay out more and more length, the farther you can sail your cast across the waiting water. But I want to say this again: When you are looping your line into the clear air, for those pure moments of fluid construction, it is an end in itself.

The cast has so many dangers, entire books have been written about them. The crocodile jawbone patterns of a sideways-slipping cast. The flop and slap of a casting motion that goes even a little past ten o'clock in front or two behind. The collapsing weight of the good cast gone unaccountably bad, loops of line simply falling down on themselves, crumbling out of the air. And my particular downfall, the sloppy misfire of slack let out too soon. The combination of naturalness and intricacy in the cast is hard to shake, that very same deceptive ease that makes golf so unnerving and evil, causing you with that one fortunate swing to believe that the game will surrender its mysteries to you, will open its mind to yours.

Not so; as I said before, it merely suits the sport for you to think this, to keep you coming back for more of that incomparable feeling when, now and then, you get it exactly right: sweet spot laid squarely on the dimpled ball, the cast improbably perfect and long and pure. The narrator in *A River Runs Through It*, describing the last mighty cast of his doomed brother, fishing his limit for the final time on their father's Montana trout stream, makes the comparison concrete: "On shore we were sure, although we could see no line, that the air above him was singing with loops of line that never touched the water but got bigger and bigger each time they passed and sang. . . . Paul's body pivoted as if he were going to drive a golf ball three hundred yards, and his arm went high into the great arc and the tip of his wand bent like a spring, and then everything sprang and sang."

And you realize again, once more, over and over: the battle is never between you and the fish, it's between you and yourself. Of course. What else?

All fishermen of sense revere Walton, for he is the early master; and he is indeed good company most of the time. His advice for baiting hooks and setting lines is practical and tart. How to dress a chub when that's all you could catch. (The secret is basting with vinegar, butter, and salt, "for this dries up the fluid watery humor with which all Chubs do abound.") How to fashion flies from bits of silk thread and pheasant feather, still the standard tools of the art. How to roll bits of bread, honey, and blood-meal into a lure irresistible to the grayling and the pike. How, above all, to choose your place and time of casting a line and bending a rod.

Still, he can be a bit thick. It's not so much Walton's piety that is grating—that, after all, is his prerogative as a spiritual man determined to link angling with religious contemplation. It is, rather, his apparent sentimentality, and a degree of what, for lack of a better word, we must call his prissiness. Walton is altogether too calm about fishing, perhaps a little too much in love with the contemplative and peaceful side of the angler's art. He doesn't get the relationship between reflection and action quite right. At the same time, he is sanguine to the point of hypocrisy about the prospect of impaling live bait on his hook or pounding a landed trout about the head to kill it while still fresh.

Ernest Hemingway, even before he became famous for the epic deep-sea battles of popular imagination, where one's feet are mauled on the chipped wood of the outboard, took issue with Walton in a little sketch on fishing for rainbow trout in the Soo, written for the *Toronto Star Weekly* in August of 1920. "Altogether it is a rough, tough, mauling game, lacking in the meditative qualities of the Izaak Walton school of angling," Hemingway said of battling the killer rainbow in Northern Ontario. "What would make a fitting Valhalla for the good fisherman when he dies would be a regular trout river with plenty of rainbow trout in it crazy for the fly." Killing fish is, after all, still killing. But more of that later.

Early on in his discussions with the converted falconer, now a dedicated member of the angling family, Walton suggests that one of fishing's many virtues is its ability to navigate an oft-remarked strait in human affairs between the demands of thought and those of deed. "And for that I shall tell you," Piscator says to his eager pupil, "that in ancient times a debate hath risen, and it remains yet unresolved, whether the happiness of man in this world doth consist more in contemplation than in action." The remark is surely meant to evoke the classical discussion in, among other places, Aristotle's *Nicomachean Ethics*. There, in the West's first great treatise on the details of human virtue, the philosopher maps out a program and procedure for those actions that will contribute to the aim of human life, the particular form of flourishing called in the Greek *eudaimonia*. The word is most often translated as "happiness" in English, but the Greek indicates something more vivid, and deeper, than the good fortune and positive feelings evoked by the relatively recent English coinage. *Eudaimonia* means something more like "attended by the beautiful spirit," blessed, fortunate, and flourishing.

That includes a measure of the things and experiences we would categorize with worldly goods. Indeed, it is sometimes surprising to modern readers how much of Aristotle's recipe for linking ethics and happiness includes often despised hedonistic pleasures and material successes: wealth and honours, luck and practical judgement. But this is a matter of emphasis. Such goods are only valuable when taken in their proper degree, and recognized for their limits.

The so-called practical syllogism—the mechanism by which virtues of thought translate judgement into action—is the keystone of the *Ethics*. It is clear that, for Aristotle and his young pupils, there is no such thing as good character without good action, and vice versa.

And yet, at the very end of this quite practical guide to life, which includes discussion of tricky examples and the virtues concerning disposition of riches, there is a destabilizing move. In the tenth and final book of the *Ethics*, Aristotle suggests that contemplation, not action, is the highest capacity of the human soul. Contemplation goes beyond the goal-oriented virtues of thought discussed earlier in the treatise, the *phronesis* of good judgement and the *theoria* of scientific investigation. Contemplation is the specific form of thought we mean when we call reflection "philosophical"—the kind of thought dedicated to no purpose other than greater awareness of who we are, a sense of *how to be here,* in the land of the mortals.

Aristotle thus confronts head-on a basic dilemma that neither he nor anyone can resolve neatly. Is it better to act or to reflect? If we act without reflection, we may do good but we will never be certain of it, because our vision will be narrow in sympathy and purpose. If we reflect but do not act, we will be wise to no purpose, leaving the world exactly as it is. Philosophy, the saying goes, bakes no bread; it does not change the world—and when it seeks to, it ceases to be philosophy and becomes politics. But few philosophers have so mastered themselves that they can forbear from all action. A state of complete contemplation might be likened to death, and there is more than one sense in which philosophy is, as famously defined, practice for death. It is, says the classicist F.M. Cornford, a world 'where the only action is thought, and thought is free from fear." Yes, but how?

Aristotle minimizes the dilemma without resolving it, saying that we must act in order to achieve the flourishing that is the purpose of all life, but that the contemplative part of our nature is the highest and most god-like and so should be cultivated. A point that lurks nearby, though Aristotle himself does not make it explicit, is that only in reflection is the true nature of the conflict between action and reflection revealed—an advantage which might suggest, paradoxically, that reflection is by definition superior to action in managing to encompass both.

And so the link to fishing. "Some have said that an angler must be a man of no thinking," wrote James Saunders in *The Complete Fisherman* of 1724. "On the other hand, I take it to be rather a token of a thinking retir'd disposition. . . He that angles, must have all his passions at his command, he must govern his temper with an absolute

sway, and be able to sustain his mind under the greates
disappointments."

No business for dummies, in other words.

In addition to Aristotle, whom he does not mention bu
certainly must have known, Walton was probably thinkin
of the celebrated poetic dyad from Milton that seems t
address the action-versus-contemplation dilemma
"L'Allegro" and "Il Penseroso" were published in 1632, tw
decades before the first edition of the *Angler*. Milton, a
apologist for the Commonwealth, was Walton's natura
political enemy, but Walton could not but have bee
impressed with the poet's wise and accomplished treatmen
of human character in its active and reflective modes.

In the first poem, Milton gives a high-spirited account o
high spirits, praising the pleasures and ambitions of youth
especially the modern transformation of rural lustiness int
the excited striving of the urban scene. "Tow'red Citie
please us then," the poet declares, "And the busy hum o
men." In "Il Penseroso," we confront an aging and sad ma
who takes pleasure instead in cloistered wandering, th
peculiar happiness of retirement and oblivion. "These pleas
ures Melancholy give," he says, "And with thee I choose t

ive." Together the poems do not so much unravel the action–thought dichotomy as suggest that these are natural stages of human life we must all go through.

Walton does not want to let the question off the hook that way. He outlines the respective claims of action and reflection and then declares himself modestly. "Concerning which two opinions," he says, "I shall forbear to add a third by declaring my own, and rest myself contented with telling you, my very worthy friend, that both these meet together, and do most properly belong to the most honest, ingenuous, quiet, and harmless art of Angling." Which, apart from once more insisting on quietness alien to the more robust, full-contact angler of today, is not really a forbearance. The dialectical synthesis of the two opinions would indeed, if valid, constitute a third opinion. Unless, that is, Walton's move is not a synthesis at all but merely a way of avoiding the clash of opinions altogether and so settling on a simpler, maybe higher truth: In fishing done properly, where hope rules over reason, there is no *conflict* between action and contemplation, and so no issue of resolution thereof.

To *hope* for something is to think actively, to think in a way that impinges on the world without being certain what the end will be, without being instrumental. The difference between the Greek conception of human nature, which until recently dominated the Western tradition, and the one we are driven to accept in a post-Darwinian age is the differ ence between closure and openness, between what philoso pher Richard Rorty calls "the security of the unchangeable" and the "romance of unpredictable change." Whatever their considerable merits, the ancient Greek notions of human flourishing were fixed and unvarying; that is why, says Aristotle, they submit to rational study. But we can see so many more options, new vistas of both uncertainty and self creation. Living in what some like to call the post-natural world—really just the layered natural world, where we can more and more alter our own genetic course—can be profoundly unsettling. But we should welcome this shift, for here is hope's country, a place where what John Dewey labelled "the great incubus" of certainty that dominates the West can finally be outpaced. "This element of romantic hope," Rorty says of such openness, "the willingness to substitute imagination for certainty, and curiosity for pride, breaks down the Greek distinction between contemplation and action."

Of course, sometimes it's not so easy to hope. Hans Georg Gadamer, the great twentieth-century master of hermeneutic philosophy, where thought and action are rejoined, was once asked whether it is true that theory and practice are the same thing. Gadamer paused. "In theory," he said, "this is true. In practice . . ."

Imagination over certainty; curiosity over pride; hope over security—these are the virtues of the angler as well as other sorts of vigorous poetic dreamers, dreamers who are doers. And this, finally, sitting not in a seminar room or a library but in a boat on the rippled lake or standing in the coursing stream—you see that *this* is what Walton means when he says fishing avoids the snare of the ancient choice between reflection and action. Fishing teaches us to dream, to find apertures of possibility in the edifice of daily life; to act by contemplating and contemplate as a way of acting. To angle is to live in hope. And just as surely, hope's contours are revealed by angling's calmness.

6

Patience

"As no man is born an artist, so no man is born an angler."
—Walton, *The Compleat Angler*

Fred is a patient teacher, which is why he's in the boat with me, the conscientious objector from Kelowna. He's also deliberate, careful, skilled, and silent. Not for the first time in recent months, I see that I have been spending too much time in the company of women. Nothing against them, couldn't love them more—bring on the emotional speculation and intimacy—but at a certain point not long ago I became aware that, for some combination of reasons not entirely clear, almost none of my best friends were men, and I miss them. I miss the peculiar comforts they offer, not so much better as more familiar than the other kind, closer to the bone.

There is something inherently restful about male silence, concentrating on achievement rather than motive. I cast. I make a mistake, usually of the predictable rookie sort. Fred offers a pointer with the expressionless look and fine lack of censure that is the preserve of all gifted artisans when dealing with overeager beginners. Otherwise we sit, mute as cowboys in the rain. Concentrating, waiting, not bored. To the outside eye, perhaps, it seems dull and life-less; we might even look as though we are doing exactly nothing. And yet, we are doing everything, all the compli-cated invisible things that fishing demands: concentrating, looking, thinking, wondering, calculating. As any baseball player will tell you, waiting is action too.

Patience

Every half-hour or so Fred and I exchanged a word, discussed tackle options in that smooth exchange of nearly incomprehensible insider tech-language that is the joy of all men, whatever the undertaking. Fly fishing is, among other things, an exercise in amateur entomology; it demands the skillful act of deceiving some creatures by imitating other ones. In this, it lies precisely, and beautifully, along the threshold between art and nature. We need to understand the insects the fish are eating before we can catch the fish by mimicking the insects: the nymphs, the newborn flies, the fat day-old mature ones. My Ontario guide, John, once stood next to me in the Grand River and picked up a subsurface rock, turning it over to display the grubs and eggs that we needed to know. Fred, catching a fish, actually produced a miniature stomach pump and extracted the contents of the trout's gut to see what insects it had been savouring.

This was not quite the complete stream-side autopsy recommended by J.C. Mottram in his indispensable volume *Fly-Fishing: Some New Arts and Mysteries* (1915), but it is nevertheless an impressive and logical extension of the project, mentioned earlier, of *thinking like the fish*. Trout may have tiny brains, and you may think you have to shrink yours to match wits with them, but unless you know what the trout wants to eat, brain or no brain, you won't know what to show it as bait. Mottram brings to the task all the precision of medical science. "The larger descending o cardiac limb will contain more recently taken food," he notes; "the ascending or pyloric limb, food which ha undergone partial digestion, and will seldom repay exami nation." With skillful use of forceps and scissors, the recen food can be examined. "Some or all of the contents should be put into a small bottle of dilute formalin, which should be carried for this purpose, so that a more careful examina tion may be made with a lens at home."

Fred was a little less surgical but no less subtle. He squeezed the mixture of water and flies from the pump to a clear plastic bottle. It was evident that most of the insect the trout had eaten were green nymphs. Silently we changed flies and cast again. This solemn dedication, the quie earnestness brought to the objectively pointless undertak ing, probably sounds funny. It isn't. It is what smart people mean by male bonding—not the noisy carousing, the exchange of boozy anecdotes, and the tag-team flirting Instead, the small happiness of shared effort and coordi nated action, with gear but not about gear, after an end a once trivial and demanding. Skill, learning, thought, grace silence. We talk of the virtue of patience in angling, but this is patience of a very special kind: active rather than passive concentrated and effortful instead of self-denying. I know this because patience is not a quality for which I am known, either within the family or elsewhere. I am, in truth, a judgemental perfectionist, and minor faults like tardiness, bad parallel parking, or inability to operate a cash register with minimum efficiency can drive me to imprecation. So I can admire, without actually being able to replicate, Fred's ability to untangle a misguided cast that has wrapped and snarled beyond all apparent saving on an irritating branch. That takes patience, which I lack. If fishing were just about that, it *would* be stupid.

There is something else in fishing—a composed and poised endurance that is necessary for the deployment and reel of the long, light lines, an odd form of stoic buoyancy oscillating constantly between excitement and stasis. It is closer, as T.H. White said, to *perseverance* than to patience as normally conceived, an activity driven by fierce but quiet desire. That is perhaps why, now that I understand what fishing is really like, I no longer consider it stupid: it is, like all hope, an embodied paradox of desire and desire's defeat. The joys of fishing are, when they come, so *thrilling*, White says, that "the fisherman fishes as the urchin eats a cream bun, from lust." Most good anglers therefore play down the excitement of the kill, precisely because it is so wonderful when it comes. Thus the average chalkstream angler, using dry flies, may cast several hundred times a day for three days and catch not a single fish, yet be perfectly happy if he manages to land one on the fourth. Mere success would weigh down the lightness of fishing, the joy of the chase—a thought whose validity we recognize without ever relinquishing the desire to win. And fish in the creel mean that the angler returns more enladen than he sets out, another idiosyncratic inversion. "The fisherman," says Morley Roberts, "is the only creature existing whose joy is an increasing burden, a heavier handicap."

Fred and I cast and reeled, flicking our rods at the hint of underwater strikes. Several times I missed the strike, or maybe it wasn't really one at all. Long moments passed with the straight lines lying motionless on the water. Suddenly I got a strike, quickly set the hook, and felt the long winding wallop of the trout taking my line and running. The loose spools of line at my feet, an amateur's indulgence to make casting easier, pulled through the metal eyes and sang as the fish fled its nasty surprise, a water nymph with a hook concealed. I let the reel run out line and then, when there was a pause, began hauling in.

The fish resisted, and I could feel, along with his half-pound weight, the terrible possibility of the line breaking, could almost sense the exact point of tensile rupture that the line contains within it, its potential weakness. Philosophers talk of *dispositional qualities,* those features of a thing that are not always apparent—the way whiteness or firmness might be—but are instead, like fragility, contained within future possible events. A china cup is only sometimes broken, but is always fragile. The line is like this: waiting to break, forever breakable, though we hope that this time, with this fish, we will merely know and not witness this. The fish tugged and ran, and I had to let out line again so it wouldn't snap. Gradually, I was drawing the little trout toward me, letting out less line and pulling in more. The first quick run is often the most intense with trout, and they can tire early. They are not wimps like chub, which many purist anglers disdain for their tendency to surrender early, but they are far less likely than the monster salmon to make multiple and unexpected runs. Still, you can't be too careful, even with little rainbow and cutthroats, and I hauled slowly against his tiring spasms of irritation and flight.

I brought the trout in close to the boat, close enough to see that it was less than a foot long and lighter than I had thought at first. Another wee scrapper. I turned to get Fred's opinion and saw now that he had been busy the whole time, casting and fighting his own prey. You think you fish alone—ultimately you *do* fish alone, all alone, because nobody but you is holding the rod—but this is a kind of shared aloneness. Is there competitiveness there, a streak of urgency? Of course not, because Fred is an *incomparably* better angler than I am or ever will be, son of a fishing family, a born outdoorsman. We wet our hands and brought our respective catches above the water and inside the gunwales of the boat. Fred's was about half again as big as mine, and he had already lost count of his catch on this bright British Columbia morning. Twenty? Twenty-five?

"The fresh smell of trout," he said, extending his hand so I could breathe in the invigorating scent of living fish, even though my own hands, already covered with the wetness, not really slimy but somehow both sticky and clean, smelled the same way. "It always reminds me of my father when he used to take me out when I was a kid."

Besides, I was already—with Fred's help—outfishing Steve in the other boat, and that was excellent. There is probably nothing more galling than being bested by your younger brother at some characteristically manly pursuit, especially if your younger brother is a weedy philosophy professor and poncey city-boy. Steve hates it, and I like that. Breaking all rules of angling decorum and brotherly regard, I shouted out a running tally and, because it's the kind of guy I am, shared some thoughts about the liminal space between art and nature, the aesthetics of skill, the theory of conjoined beauty and use.

"I'm not listening to you, Mark," Steve called back.

That is what my brothers invariably say when I go into what they like to call "geek mode" and make some distinction or argument they haven't heard before. This is always a bit rich coming from Steve, in particular, since he is, among other things, a graduate-degree engineer who has been known to have the following kind of conversation as we drove to a golf course on Antigua one Christmas with our Uncle Bryan, who operates some resort hotels in the Caribbean:

Mark (in the back seat eating a peanut-butter-and-banana sandwich): "I wonder how big this island is."

Steve (in the front seat looking out the window): "Mark, the island of Antigua is about twelve miles across. It is of irregular shape, but let's assume it is a notional circle. What is its area?"

Mark: "Um, let's see. Area of a circle is πr^2, right? So it's, uh, the square of six times—what?—3.14 or whatever. Let's say approximately three times thirty-six, so—wait—a hundred and . . ."

Steve: "A hundred and eight square miles. Actually a bit over that, more like a hundred and thirteen. What about the circumference?"

This was reminiscent of, and yet decidedly less pleasant than, a conversation we'd had the night before while drinking martinis. I had idly wondered, not for the first time,

how much of the height of the traditional martini glass's
cone was equal to half its volume. You know, you're drinking one of those drinks and you look at the shape, and of
course you know its volume is much larger on top, where
the cone is widest. And yet it's deceptive, isn't it, how
quickly the level of the liquid drops. So you wonder how
this works, exactly. Because you think you've had only a few
sips but they're up there at the maximum extension of the
cone, aren't they, and obviously half the drink comes—or
goes—well before you're halfway down the *glass* and soon,
before you have time to calculate π to ten or so decimal
places, you're, you know, drunk. Plastered. Toasted. π-eyed.
Bahahaha.

So anyway, what *is* the shifting ratio of descending height
to volume? Harder to figure than it looks, for one thing. Be
my guest: think about this next time you're drinking a
martini. Here's a little help: the formula for volume of a
cone is $1/3\pi r^2 h$, or exactly one-third the volume of a cylin-
der of the same height and radius. Cool, huh? Now you can
do the math. Go on. That's right: half the volume of your
drink is contained in something like just over one-sixth the
top-end height of the container part of the glass, depending
on the slant of the cone at its open end, which diminishes
the volume so . . . well, never mind. And I know it sounds
wrong but it's right. One-sixth is half. If you don't believe

me, try taking your martini glass and pouring it out into two other glasses. Well, no, don't do that.

Mark (in the car): "Circumference? Well, $2\pi r$. Where r equals six miles again, so about, um, thirty-eight miles around. Something like that?"

Steve: "Yeah, more or less."

Mark: "But a coastline is a fractal, right, because of irregularities. Even if you wanted to measure it for a chart, you'd have to make an assumption of relevant scale. You're not going to count every tiny cove and inlet, because the coastline is *infinitely* long if you do. So any circumference value, no matter how accurate, is an approximation. In fact, if you start thinking about measurement the way Wittgenstein did, you see that any measurement is scheme-relative and practice-dependent! A line measured in inches is not *better* measured in microns, just 'more accurately' measured, and even then the invoked notion of 'accuracy' only makes sense for certain purposes. You know? What if a measurement in microns is of no use to me? It's not that the micron measurement gets closer to some *final* truth about the length of the line. There is no final truth lurking there, *behind* the line. There is only the line *as we measure it for our purposes*."

Steve (wearily): "A *circle,* Mark. I said a notional *circle*. Not a line. And notional circles are not fractal. Just like π is not a number."

Mark: "You're missing the poi—Wait, what do you mean, π is not a number? Of course π is a number."

Steve: "No, it's a symbol. It expresses the relationship between circumference and radius, C over r, approximately twenty-two over seven. But it's not a number, any more than the square root of two is a number. That's why they both go on infinitely when you try to give them numerical value."

Mark: "But the root of two is a number too, just an *irrational* number. Are you saying that the only real numbers are rational numbers? Are you crazy?"

Steve: "Mark, π is a symbol, or a concept. Not a number."

Mark: "Of course it's a number."

Steve: "I'm not listening to you, Mark."

You're not supposed to stand in a rowboat, but in order to cast effectively, I must. Luckily I have good balance and Fred offers placid and amiable ballast at the other end where he's sitting down and spooling out long elegant casts with no visible sign of effort or thought.

I now found myself, against all odds, entirely happy, miles from my computer or the nearest library, untroubled by philosophical arguments I need to untangle or positions I need to defend. The state of mind peculiar to fishing, which I have called reflection, is neither precisely analytical nor entirely aimless; rather, it's a happy wandering that may outwardly resemble calm yet inwardly accommodates the most felicitous meanders, a quivering suspension in the delights of the moment. You are there but not there, concentrating but immobile, sharp-eyed but relaxed. Fishing is as close to perfect mental equilibrium as a mortal may wish to approach, it seems to me, since the asymptotic end point it sketches is probably indistinguishable from an out-of-body experience or, indeed, death. It is, says one devotee, a sport "capable of reducing the most inquiring mind to the happy indifference of a turnip." And how determinedly do we seek that vegetative state of contentment, this oddly welcome fever of peace, this therapeutic disease.

There is—for all that happiness is an active state of mind—little here of the normal agitations of thought, the restless linear pursuits of logic or the frets and yearnings of worry. Nevertheless, there are proximate dangers seething, like hungry fish, beneath the calm waters of the mental lake. Anglers speak freely and in appalled tones of how the passion for fishing may run amok, of the runaway obsessive interest that eventually becomes ruinous to both finances and relationships. The beckoning mouth of the trout sings a siren song leading to addiction and, finally, a divine, destructive madness. One relieved casual angler, otherwise given to excess in all things, counted himself lucky to have avoided the disease we might call *ichthyomania* through sheer incompetence, "a blessing in disguise, like the man prevented from becoming a lush because he could never hold down the stuff."

I am far too near the beginning to feel this tow of delicious craziness, but I see already wisdom in the observation that "the man who has discovered fishing counts the world well lost." Adrift in a happiness without higher purpose, occupied but not directed, my thoughts veer off in random directions. I looked around and suddenly felt for the first time as if I were inside my country's money—the old kind, anyway, with the loons and woods, and, yes, the slow, low flight of a surprisingly massive osprey over the lake's slight chop. I thought about that day I graduated from high school and, for no good reason, avoided the injuries that so easily could have ended my young life. The face of an old girlfriend, one of those mad beautiful heartbreakers your friends warn you against, swam up from memory. I thought of my ex-wife, whom I miss in ways I still hardly understand.

It began to rain. I remember a postcard she sent me a long time ago, before everything changed, inscribed with some lines from Donne: "Where, like a pillow on a bed, / A pregnant bank swelled up, to rest / The violet's reclining head, / Sat we two, one another's best."

Which was true, at the time.

Cast and wait; reel slowly in. Cast and wait. Pull the line. We were once more fishing wet flies. The easier casts were giving me a sense of accomplishment I knew would be instantly obliterated if I were trying the same thing with dry flies. Also, we were on a lake, not in a stream, and that helped. We had the boat to anchor us, an unsubtle but useful platform of stability, rather than the tricky wading among rocks and reeds. Also we had lake-born rainbows, not the less plentiful and, you know, *smarter* trout who populate the brooks.

Casting well, especially when you're a relative beginner, requires that strange form of anxious boldness familiar from, say, diving off a five-metre platform the first time or slugging back your first neat whisky. Riding a motorbike. Driving for the basket from the top of the key. Breaking down a door. There should be a name for this class of ordinary actions where the worst thing you can be is tentative. When casting, if you don't snap the rod sharply back and forth, pausing at the end of each movement to let the line sing, you won't get the loops growing in the air around you. You have to make yourself forget there is a hook on the end of the line, a small barb capable of lodging in your eye—or Fred's.

My cast slipped a little bit sideways—I let my wrist break over—but I still managed to get a good length of line on the water. I know it's a wet-fly cast and nothing to tell *Field and Stream* about, but still: *success is an event.* I stood in the boat, line extended, rod pointed down and out toward where the fly had landed and sunk below the surface. A few minutes passed and I felt the slight tug on the end that said a decent-sized rainbow trout was hitting my fly. A quick flip of the lovely light rod, up and to the right, and the tiny hook was set. After casting, setting the hook is probably the hardest part of fly fishing, an action where a certain natural talent is necessary. I seem to be good at this—quick-draw reflexes, gunslinger quickness, something—and this makes me very happy.

Rainbow trout, even little ones under a foot long, are fighters. They're not as picky as brown trout or as wily as brook, but they like to scrap. When you have one on the line, you know it. I pulled in my slack as fast as I could and kept the rod high to maintain tension, bending it into the beautiful iconic bow so lovingly described by Walton. The hooked rainbow trout leapt five feet above the lake surface in a moment that was incomparably exhilarating, mythical, almost pre-scripted. *Fish are jumpin'!* Like all things long imagined but rarely experienced, an accretion of literary or cinematic associations, you can't quite believe it's really there, your fish, hooked and angry, leaping and writhing on the line forty feet away. You have to keep the battling fish in front of you, because if it swims under the boat, you are in all kinds of trouble with the suddenly slack line and the leader tangling in the engine or undergrowth.

Gradually I pulled him in, using my left hand to haul the line while my right index finger held it tight against the quivering rod. If the line goes slack, the hook, with its virtually non-existent barb, will come loose. The fish leapt again. He was dark and big, with a blunt head and a slash of red showing at the gills—a foot long or more. I held the line and pulled. I kept the rod straight. Whether he likes it or not, I thought, I'm bringing him in. Especially if he doesn't like it.

Now he was tired and angry, but I had him held tight alongside the boat with the rod tense and firm in my right hand. This was tricky, all right. Our rule for catch and release angling is that you have to touch the fish for it to count, and ideally bring it inside the gunwales of the boat. We don't use nets because that would make it too easy.

Holding the rod in my right hand, line kept tight, I crouched down and tried to grab the nearly invisible leader line with my left. The fish, definitely twelve inches at least and so maybe just over a pound, predictably decided this moment of vulnerability on my part was a good time to start fighting again. Like a character in an overwrought action movie, I missed grabbing the flailing line about four times before I finally got a grip.

At that point, I had a real problem. My hands were full and the fish was just sitting there in the water, hooked. I needed another hand to make another move, to lift him out of the water. I've seen anglers put their flyweight rods between their teeth at this point, freeing up a hand to deal with the fish. Not trusting myself to complete that kind of professional manoeuvre, I slid my hand down the line until it was right by the fish's head. He was caught nicely on the lip, not an ugly snag deep in the throat or a brutal one on the cheek or eye, and the release should have been smooth. If I could get hold of him, that is. In one slightly spastic motion, I got the hook in my left hand and dropped the long rod, bringing my right hand into the water and around his fat body. This was a lot harder than it sounds, since I was at this point bent more than double over the steel gunwale of the small boat, panting with excitement and the fear of losing my biggest fish of the day.

Fred, in case you were wondering, was still fishing away and offering occasional, not-very-helpful hints. "Grab him," he said. "Don't let go." Right.

The battling trout went calm when my hand closed lightly around his middle, as they often do. I lifted him gently out of the water and, for the brief but essential moment, brought him inside the boat, our little bubble of tools and artificiality. I removed the tiny hook by flipping my left hand over, grasped the fish with two hands, and had my first proper look since the strike. It was a lovely fish, a mature fat rainbow, dark on top and beautifully coloured along its thick sides, big enough for Fred to snap a picture with the little camera we'd brought along. The developed picture would prove to cut out much of the fish from the frame, leading to endless disputes about its actual size. Naturally.

I put him back in the water, made a few waves through his gills to revive him, and he was back in play. Some catch-and-release anglers will thank their prey out loud for the sport, but that seemed a smidge pious for me. I thanked him silently instead.

And then I cast again.

7

Killing

"For I am not of a cruel nature—I love
to kill nothing but fish."
—Walton, *The Compleat Angler*

Catch & Release

Y ou're supposed to have a club or something for killing the fish—a short wooden bat is probably best—so you can deliver the quick sharp blow to the side of its head that breaks the little spine and stops the slow gill-flapping agony of above-the-surface suffocation. Sean and I, in our boat on the lake near Kelowna, didn't have a club or a stone or anything, really, suitable for killing a flopping trout with the smart deliberate stroke that is the only respite from its ordeal. The reason for this is good enough, because we were out there just fishing, catching and releasing, and nobody seriously thought about killing the damn things when what we mostly do is throw them back. But I was leaving the next day and I suddenly had a craving for the sweet delicate pink flesh of freshwater trout, packed tight in dense flakes.

You can see why. These days the trout I see, when I see them at all, are pan-seared or flash-broiled or quick-grilled, accompanied by, who knows, boysenberry compote or chopped-fig-and-olive tapenade, served with a medley of blanched seasonal root vegetables or on a bed of organic baby greens. I mean, I usually see trout, if I see them at all, all gussied up and tidy, boneless and beguiling, on some high-piled plate of downtown evening artistry, some twenty-five-year-old cokehead culinary genius's version of creativity set before me with a reverent flourish and a thirty-dollar price tag. Faugh.

Killing

I want it the other way, hooked and cleaned and quick-filleted, dunked in salt-and-pepper flour and tossed into a heavy, carbon-encrusted skillet and fried up within an hour of coming out of the cold cold water. I want greasy scrambled eggs and bacon alongside, lots of black coffee, and a stack of unbuttered toast. I want to eat it all so fast, because I'm ravenous from being out since six in the morning, that I only register just how good it was afterward, like a retinal image that flashes on the inside of my eyelid—on, off, on, off—when the light source has gone.

Most of all, I want the fish I eat to be the fish I caught. My fish. The one who answered my flicking cast, who was fooled by my little green fly. The fish whose own hunger made him strike at the twist of green thread and bits of feather that resembled, just enough, a post-larval mayfly, but had, inside the deceit, a tiny hook with an even more minuscule barb. The fish that then struggled, leaping and zagging and twisting, to rid itself of the pulling, persistent invader in its lower lip. The fish that lost that little battle between me and it, and then, after the way of things, lost its life when I managed to haul it inside the boat and transform it from living, breathing fish into breakfast.

Before all that, though, we have to kill the trout right here on the line. Obviously we have to kill it. There are only a few kinds of food we eat while they're still alive and trout isn't one of them. The fish, unhooked from the line, is flopping around in the swill of dirty water and spilled beer that is the bilge of our small boat.

Sean said, "Mark, we have to kill it."

"Okay," I said, meaning, *Go ahead.*

Sean hesitated for just a second and then broke off a piece of wood from a dead tree in the stand of naked pines where we were anchored. He steadied the fish around the middle of its fat body and raised the makeshift club—too light, really, and too crooked for the job at hand. He brought it down quickly and struck the trout somewhere just back of its blunt head.

It was a good swift blow, despite the awkwardness of the instrument. The trout, a foot-long rainbow, lay still. We both sat back. But then, after a long moment, the fish began to flop again, this time in apparent slow motion. It was not dead. The mouth was still gaping open and closed in that dumb, affecting way fish have: *Help me, help me.* Its spinal cord apparently still functional, its tiny brain still sending messages along the short central nervous system, saying (we can only imagine), *Air! Air!* and *Get me the hell out of here!*

"Shit," Sean said. He picked up the broken-off branch again and took the trout in hand to deliver another smack, this one with a shorter upswing and more heft. The wood slammed the fish's body against the metal hull of the boat and its thrashing form went completely still, the beautiful fanned tail now angled slightly up toward the sky. Sean pulled the branch away and revealed the freshly crushed head of the trout, its left eye dislodged and bloody, a squirt of pink and dark red running under the body and mixing lazily with the water and beer and other grunge in the runnels of the boat.

"Jesus, Sean," I said. We both laughed uneasily.

"Better that than letting it die slowly," he said, which was true.

We went back to our rods, reeled the line in, and made to cast again. The trout, when we ate it later, was delicious.

Debate continues over the ethics of fishing, influenced by periodic reports of evidence that fish must feel pain, and reports of counter-evidence that their brains lack the complexity to do any such thing. Whatever the merits of the scientific findings, I was inclined to dislike angling, if not quite disapprove outright, from well before that first night in Kelowna three years ago. Fishing is not just stupid, I thought, but *bad*. Lord Byron, for instance, though lacking the authority of neurological research, was nevertheless uncompromising; he called it the "cruelest, coldest and stupidest of pretended sports," and concluded that "no angler can be a good man." His assessment of poor Walton, who did talk some awful tosh about treating gently the live frogs through which he drew his bait hook, is that the tables should be turned. These lines appear in a note to *Don Juan*, Canto xiii:

And angling, too, that solitary vice
Whatever Izaak Walton sings or says
The quaint, old, cruel coxcomb, in his gullet
Should have a hook, and a small trout to pull it.

Whether or not we take the poet at his word—as one critic has noted, Byron's indignation is "expressed in a work, the hero of which is a model of refined cruelty," never restricting himself to "solitary vice" but indulging the much more public ones of adultery, gambling, and intrigue—he has a point. For all Walton's talk of gentleness and calm, he is a murderer of fish for sport. Can this be all right? Viscount Grey articulates the standard view when he says, confidently, that the only intimate danger to the fish in angling is a little fear, since they are cold-blooded and feel no pain. Or, as Grey's contemporary A.H. Chaytor put it, "A great accumulation of instances in which fish seem to have shown an almost complete indifference to wounds or injuries that would cause extreme agony to warm-blooded animals, seems to establish as a fact that fish are comparatively insensible to pain."

But note the number of argument-weakening qualifications: *almost complete; seems to establish; comparatively insensible*. Most basically, this position betrays an implicit anthropomorphism. Why should we consider a lack of mammalian behavioural response, even if that were indeed an established fact, which it is not, as evidence of insensibility to pain? Any philosopher will tell you that it is in principle impossible to know such a thing, and, anyway, the struggling fish certainly does give every outward impression of reacting with an impressive combination of fear, panic, pain, and anger. It will apparently do anything it can think of to get rid of a hook. It is hardly indifferent to the hook's presence in its mouth. There would, after all, be no such thing as fishing if it were. You might as well, proverbially, dynamite the lake or take your firearm to a barrel.

It is unlikely that fish feel no pain or discomfort *at all*, then, though their experience of those states must surely lack the complexity of ours. So, let us grant for the sake of argument and our consciences that they do not feel the intensity of what we know as pain. Nevertheless, fish show clear signs of distress when they are hooked and fought by anglers. Is that a defensible sport? Fanciers of fishing typically assert that the fish's struggle is actually proof *against* the presence of pain, especially in a fish that has been caught and released or has snapped off a hook and leader. It would not, after all, willingly return to the source of its agony if it were really so bad.

But this is nonsense too, since the whole art of fly fishing lies in deceiving the fish into thinking the fly with its secret hook is just a fly, not a proximate instrument of death. If fish were not fooled by flies, fly fishing would not be much sport. If they were so dumb that they rose and struck even knowing the hook was there, we would be dumber still for matching wits against them. We can hardly use the trout's own desire for food and inability to tell real from artificial against him, since they are the very things upon which angling relies.

At this point, the position tends to circle back on itself. Anglers will say that it is the battle itself that justifies their pursuit. The fish killed at the end of a fly line dies because of its own hunger, aggression, or greed, yes. But it has the choice not to strike, and so dies *freely* in an even contest with the angler, who, on a chalkstream anyway, might count himself lucky to win two or three times in a day. The fine-tuning of angling to greater degrees of lightness and difficulty is not merely the invidious distinction of a class system but also, more crucially, a levelling of the playing field. It nakes the trout harder to get, and so the angler harder to condemn.

I am inclined to accept that argument, more or less, though I suspect others will not—or not yet, since it sometimes takes a day or two on lake or stream before you realize just how hard it can be to land a fish. Also how satisfying, and how human.

This is the bullet we should bite: fishing is not just permissible but fun, and fun because it is relaxing and thrilling at once. Though catch and release is arguably a more humane version of angling than catch and keep, especially when one cannot reasonably eat more than a trout a day, it should be remembered that we mostly practise catch and release so the fishing will continue to be good, not because we think killing fish absolutely morally wrong. We have the option, each time, of deciding that a given fish is a keeper—which is to say, a goner. The sport is poised, once more, on a fulcrum of deep notions. We do not precisely *need* the fish for food, and so we are indulging a sport. ("We are civilized men, not merely fishers for meat," Roderick Haig-Brown wrote.) And yet, the essence of the sport is tangled up in its original utility in landing dinner. We fish because we can, not because we have to—but fishing reminds us, should we have to, that we can.

Catch & Release

Those of us who eat fish regularly should not shy away from the ethical choices we have made in so doing. There are ethical-purist anglers who, like reformed hunters who replace their gun barrels with telephoto lenses, count themselves satisfied with a strike on their line, surrendering the need even to catch the fish. But this strikes most other anglers, myself included, as rather poor sport. If we are going to take joy in fishing, catching fish, and sometimes killing them, we can't be so shy. And so the morality of angling seems to me finally to swing back the other way. From the point of view of honesty and integrity, fishing is actually superior to eating fish without knowing how to dress tackle, cast, set, and play the tasty trout into your creel. One of the deep joys of fishing is this little return to primitive competence, the satisfying jolt of *killing for food*, and seeing death up close.

It is an experience more people should have, really. Sixty percent of Canadians live in the country's nine largest cities and experience a life where death is never absent, but always, when possible, tamed; people sometimes speak of cities as places where violent death is common, but in fact the opposite is true. Between town and country there is no contest on this point: bloody demise is a much more visible fact of life away from the streets and avenues of our downtown homes, in the fields and streams, the forests and lakes of exurbia. And that is especially true of the daily death necessary for our three meals. More than this, there is a sense of distance that opens up in the big cities, where everything is possible and nothing is unavailable. All your needs are catered for, there is no urgency finally to know how to *do* anything. There is always a guy, or a shop, or a delivery service, that can hook you up. Doing whatever it is we do—manipulating symbols, punching keyboards, sketching figures in the air—most of us are no longer capable of doing the things our ancestors of even a century ago took for granted as basic abilities.

This is an old point, but a pressing one. In New York, I often thought, the feeling is even stronger than in other places, even other cities, since the underlying idea of New York seems to be that it is expressly built to free you—which is to say, in truth, a lucky few of us—from every kind of daily care. Goods and services of all imaginable variety can arrive at your door within scant minutes of your forming a desire. If you have the money, your wish is the city's command. And contrary to myth, it doesn't actually take all that much money. The pressure of competition makes Manhattan a controlled experiment in classical economic models, demand forcing prices down and down.

Don't get me wrong: especially for a bachelor with no liking for most domestic tasks (cooking ever the exception, though applied selectively), it's great to drop off a bag of dirty laundry and get it back, cleaned, pressed, and folded, an hour later and for a couple of dollars a pound. If you were so inclined, you could live your entire life in an apartment, ordering food and movies and books and anything you wanted by phone or website.

But this triumph of urban servicing is the evolutionary equivalent of the Peter Principle. We have advanced beyond the level of our own competence, spinning ever more elaborate infrastructures that are at once miraculous and fragile, brittle edifices of spun sugar and ingenuity. And, as nature or terrorists every now and then remind us, it takes very little to cause a chunk of that confection to come crumbling down. Our grief, rage, and frustration when it does—our inability to cope with a snarled airline schedule or grid-locked intersection—is a sad clue to our own dependency and despair, which most of us are content to ignore when the smooth flow of transactional life has been restored. But we should perhaps be less hasty to return to the universe of unreflective movement and satisfaction.

To angle is not exactly to *escape* from the reach of technology, the multi-node network of modernity's grid, for there is little or nothing in our lives that actually does allow such escape, enforced simplicity and back-to-earth fetishists notwithstanding. In fishing there is always gear, the refined products of sporting death: from split-cane to fibreglass to carbon; from catgut to horsehair to nylon. But it is wrong to see angling as just the city by other means, as I once did, an unequal battle between humans and fish. Angling is as close to zero-degree technology as we are likely to get in a complex world. A rod, a line, a hook. It doesn't often get as basic as that. And even if you are, like us, catching and releasing, it's always good to keep a couple for eating, just to remind yourself that you could, maybe, if you had to, get your own dinner from the wide open expanse of the natural world.

You can try, anyway.

Every fisherman, as I said before, is familiar with the combination of quiet and frenzy that is typical of his sport. Long bouts of waiting give way without warning to bursts of adrenalized excitement, and the successful shift from one to the other is one of the things that marks a good angler from someone who simply dangles a line in the water.

In freshwater fishing, this transition can be frequent enough to make it feel as if one is always in action, casting and waiting, hauling line, and—on a good day—fighting fish. If things are going well, it can feel like non-stop activity, opening up none of the space for reflection that we thoughtful (and, let's be honest, occasionally unlucky) anglers have always praised as part of the sport. But even here, the floating dry fly or bright orange marker of a submerged wet fly can lie so long upon the sparkling water that the mind wanders off into mazes of reverie, a parade of memories and half-formed thoughts, a state of being we might be inclined to call boredom were it not so contented and so lacking in the cramped restlessness—the need to escape inactivity—that is the mark of boredom. But more about boredom later.

In deep-sea fishing, I found, the mixture of action and inaction is even more pronounced and dreamy, and the killing is that much more graphic when it happens. One winter, soon after I'd been fishing for a couple of years, Steve and I spent that Christmas in Antigua where our uncle, Bryan, operates his fabulous hotels.

Bryan is our mother's sister's husband, a funny guy's guy who grew up in Toronto's Junction neighbourhood and has spent an inordinate amount of time in the Caribbean for somebody who hates the sun so much. His nickname in the family is JTM—jokes too much—after the time he made Sean cry from relentless teasing. Our Aunt Liz—Auntie—is a tiny society lady who looks younger every year and loves to give and go to parties. In the mid-seventies my brothers and I, refugees from hot mosquito-infested Winnipeg, used to spend summers at their place in Mississauga, where there was a pool. My most vivid memories of those sojourns are of endless invented games in the pool, daily trips to the mall in my aunt's boxy green Parisienne, and watching Auntie's favourite show, *The A-Team*. You can't imagine how incomparably funny it is to hear a pretty Mississauga matron, dressed in her satin caftan and drinking a white wine spritzer, imitate Mr. T.

Refugees again, this time from Boston and Toronto, Steve and I were visiting this new haven. Steve's wife, Jaimie, and their daughter, Aidan, were also there. (Aidan, not yet four, had overheard and mastered the JTM tag, which we all found hilarious.) It was a full house when we were all gathered for meals, a sea of chatter and jokes and planning; there was no silence and almost no solitude. A welcome shock, then, for Steve and me to find ourselves in early-morning muteness, heading out to open sea from St. George's Harbour with Derek Biel, the outrigger's German captain, and his Antiguan mate, Buchan—who, implausibly, has an aunt in Winnipeg.

I was financing my share of this fishing charter with winnings from casino blackjack, amassed crudely if effectively the evening before while smoking a cigar, drinking scotch, and pretending to be cool. Steve and Bryan, allegedly better players, had both ended up losing money, which they assured me was at least partly owing to my unorthodox play messing up the card shoe. So I was feeling good as we slammed into the windward chop of the sea, Montserrat and Guadeloupe both visible in the haze to the south. It was a fine clear day, hot and almost cloudless, with the steady easterly breeze Antiguans call the "Christmas winds." The gorgeous harbour, with its towering masts and rainbow of pennants, receded gradually. We passed the resort, next bay over from the marina, then hit open water.

The boat was small but beautifully equipped, with six rods baited and arrayed along the stern and gunwales, two running through the outriggers and all set to troll at different depths and lengths. In the middle, bolted heavily to the boat, was the semi-mythical chair, familiar again from books and movies, where you strap yourself in and haul the line with a reel as big as your head. Steve and I decided we would take turns taking the chair if there were any hits. As it turned out, it wasn't that simple. Deep-sea fishing charters are odd ventures. The captain is taking you out for sport, which he may or may not be able to deliver. But he's also looking to catch fish, which, assuming you can't take them all, he will sell on the dock. You both want to catch fish but for somewhat different motives, and this colours the experience. He's almost certainly a better fisherman than ou are. But, on the other hand, you're paying *him* for the privilege of maybe losing a fish he would otherwise catch.

Luckily we didn't have that problem. The first couple of strikes, just a few minutes out, were barracuda, two or three feet long. This gave Steve and me our first experience of jumping into the chair and hauling the flagpole rods and massive reels of deep-sea fishing. The chair is built just as you would expect, with a slot for the rod between your legs and a stout footboard for you to press on as you reel. The captain slams the boat into neutral as soon as there is a strike, and the mate jumps to grab the rod and get it over to you as you climb awkwardly into the chair.

Even with a little fish like a barracuda, it is surprisingly hard to haul. The reel is low and awkward, the boat is pitching and rolling despite the beautiful day, and you can feel the adrenaline pumping through your arms and legs. When it's over, which is quickly if you're hauling properly, keeping the line tight, your limbs are quivering with strain and natural chemicals. I looked a bit longingly after my first barracuda, a rangy, muscular bastard with those awesome razoring teeth, as the mate tossed it back into the water. "We're after bigger than that," Derek said to me, but I thought, *What if that's all we get?* I knew barracuda wasn't good eating, but that fearsome-looking thing was still the biggest single fish I'd ever had on a line.

Then, as so often, a long stretch of nothingness. The sun beat down and the four of us gazed silently into the retreating ocean for a sluggish hour. And, suddenly, a big strike and it was Steve's turn in the chair. The line was pulled straight out of the back of the boat and into the middle distance, singing high, as Buchan scrambled to clear the other rods so they wouldn't foul on the strike. Steve was now hauling and lifting, hauling and lifting, like a clean-and-jerk weightlifter. Then, amazingly, the huge fish broke the water, like something out of every Hemingway-envy dream you've ever had. It was a wahoo, a big silver-grey slab of muscle with a small ventral sailfin and a razor-sharp mouth. Four feet long, maybe more.

Steve hauled and reeled. Derek, jumping down from the flying bridge with impressive lightness for so big a man, was shouting orders I couldn't understand as he and Buchan rushed around the tiny back deck to help land this struggling behemoth. They grabbed a big gaff and what looked like a small baseball bat with a loop of leather thong knotted through a hole in the handle. Steve had by then reeled the wahoo hard in close to the stern and held him, tired and frustrated, and Derek leaned over and gaffed it expertly just behind the head, hauling it up and over the stern. He gave it to Steve, passing over the whole fish-and-gaff armful, and Steve posed for a photograph while still looking somewhat shell-shocked and shaky from the fight. I snapped the photo and he dropped the massive fish to the deck. Buchan leaned over casually and killed it with one quick blow behind the head, then manhandled it into the ice locker, where it just fit. Five feet, easy.

Actually, okay, more like four. But it looked huge and sounded even bigger as it thrashed around the locker in a few final death spasms.

The next strike was mine and I seriously wondered if I could manage it. The same frenzy of awkward activity in the pitching boat, banging my knee hard as I climbed into the chair, then reeled and lifted for all I was worth. This was *hard*. I could feel the strain on my lungs and heart. "Don't fight him," Buchan said. "Just reel him quickly in." No problem. A small portion of my mind found time to question the coherence of this advice, but I just cranked the reel as hard as I could, holding the thick rod up in my left hand to keep the line tight. My feet were pressing on the board beneath them, as if it were the floor of a car driven by my aunt through the narrow streets of Antigua while I sat terrified in the passenger seat. I could feel the thigh muscles bulging, my body quivering with effort.

The fish jumped, and I wanted to take a pause-button moment to pump a fist in the air at this longed-for, this epic sight, but (a) I can't stop time, and (b) even if I could, I only have two hands and they were both heavily occupied. It wasn't a wahoo this time, but the blunt head and lemon-lime body of a dolphin fish, or mahi mahi. It was big, maybe three feet, but not like the wahoo. On the other hand, it was a lot prettier. "Stop reeling," Derek said, as I felt my forearm muscles burn. He leaned over to gaff the fish and bring it in, hauled it over the stern, and handed the gaff to me. "Better get a picture before the colours fade," he said. Dolphin fish are absolutely gorgeous, like fish-tank beauties grown to massive size, iridescent greens and yellows slashing along their odd hump-headed bodies. As with marlin, whose luminous blue fades to grey in scant minutes after death, dolphin drain colour as they expire. I said to Steve, "I guess that's what happens when you *kill* things."

Now, though, there was sudden chaos on the little deck. Three strikes in about five minutes. Steve was in the chair and the captain had taken one rod for himself. The mate was helping me haul line on a rod fixed on the starboard gunwale, a small wahoo hooked there. If reeling while in the chair is difficult, reeling while bending over the rod is nearly impossible. I strained at the reel, winding in what seemed like a mile of line, and finally got the little wahoo, maybe two-thirds the size of the first one, close enough for us to grab with the gaff.

Killing

Steve, meanwhile, had landed a biggish dolphin, which was now flopping around the deck, bleeding from the gaff wound. Blood and brine splattered on our shoes and legs; the deck ran with gore. Derek had already climbed back to the bridge and engaged the engine. Buchan was sort of herding the dolphin with his feet, trying to get a good blow with the bat. The fish flopped and bled, spraying pink fluid everywhere. Finally Buchan gaffed it again and quickly tossed it into the ice locker to join the other victims, where, not dead yet, its frenzied side-to-side slams could be heard for another ten minutes. Within a minute, Buchan had hosed away all evidence of this violent death, re-baited the hooks, and assumed once more his calm position at the top of the gangway.

We were now following a pilot bird, a massive seagull relative whose lazy sweeps track the schools of mahi mahi and wahoo. Derek circled and circled, tracing lines back and forth across the ocean, eyes heavenward all the while, watching his unwitting guide. Good fishing takes luck, but it also takes guile, and sometimes you mimic the predator as well as the prey. In the end we caught six dolphin fish and the two wahoo, not to mention the three barracudas we threw back. But after the frenzy of the three strikes, the morning tailed off into sun-baked inaction. Two more strikes, long minutes apart, and then nothing for an hour. Two hours.

Steve and I, sitting or standing on the deck, sometimes talked—about our respective friends, our plans for the coming year—but mostly just stared silently into the ocean. Stared and stared and thought about who knows what. An oil tanker distant in the haze. Tracking the progress of sailboats heading out from Guadeloupe. Five hours on the ocean and perhaps fifteen minutes of action in total. But you don't know that, and so every minute of inaction is one in which you might suddenly hear Derek pop the engine into neutral and begin barking orders in his odd German-Antiguan English, a minute that might bring more blood running onto the deck. And it is a fine day's catch.

We returned to St. George's at about one in the afternoon. As we approached the outer harbour, Derek threw the engines ahead full, the outriggers came in, and the boat sat up another few feet in the water, digging its stern screws down into a deep frothy furrow and planing the bow up above the turquoise sea with purest speed. Into the marina, and Steve and I jumped from the boat to meet Uncle Bryan. The three of us watched as Derek laid out the eight big fish we had caught, an impressive haul for half a day. People on the dock came down to have a look and offered to take our picture. This felt strange, since all we'd really done was sit in a chair and defeat fish by main force. There is not enough sport here, somehow, I thought, and not just because of the bloody demise, the harsh difference from gentle catch and release. The art of this fishing, such as it is, lies with the captain: his boat, his bait, his lines, his cruising. And, of course, his art lies in turn with that of the bird, following nature's signpost. This is fun, but it is, despite the effort, too certain, too utilitarian, too much like work. There is space for thought here, yes, but no sense of equilibrium, no settling into the natural world of the fish you seek.

We couldn't eat all those fish, not even close, so we took fillets off just one of the mahi mahi and left it at that. Wahoo is good to eat, meaty and hearty, but dolphin fish is excellent, a tender and juicy white flesh that is somehow both delicate and firm. I knew that this would be even better than the best stuff I'd had in restaurants. Just out of the ocean, cut into slabs, grilled later that same day with just salt and pepper and a little olive oil, then a few lime wedges squeezed over it. Yes.

We caught it; we killed it; we ate it. And it was delicious. But there was something essential missing—maybe the gratitude and depth that attends the chase for trout. Or do I just mean that it was not *elegant,* that it lacked the justifying feature of catch-and-release angling, of so many of life's undertakings—namely, a sense of beauty.

8

Boredom, Procrastination, and Losing Your Way

"Most of us live wherever circumstances decide that we should, and live the life that our work requires. We think of our pleasures in night watches, in passing from one place to another, upon the pavement, in trains and cabs . . ."

—Viscount Grey, *Fly Fishing*

You might think you'd get tired of casting and reeling, catching and releasing, over and over, hours on end, but I can assure you that you don't.

Grey notes how hard it is to convey this joy, and how pallid one's language becomes when attempting to recount a good day's fishing. It is, he says, like trying to describe "last year's clouds." And so the cynical choose to believe that there is nothing there to describe, as if the pleasure of angling is a grand conspiracy maintained by devotees for obscure reasons known only to themselves. Not so, Grey assures us, quite correctly; it is rather that, as so often with matters of deep satisfaction, the joy of fishing simply escapes the limits of language. Every time we seek to communicate it, we fail—fail both ourselves and it. Perhaps better not to try, therefore, and so not to fail, for that will render the cynical objection moot, with the added benefit of leaving the subject of fishing in the hands of those who enjoy it rather than judge it.

To be sure, Grey did not take his own advice. Rather, in giving it, in his graceful little book on fishing the streams of Scotland and England, he succeeds only, paradoxically, in refuting it: the book, precisely by forswearing the task of persuasion, manages to persuade. Which is a neat trick and pretty much the standard operating procedure for all writing that means to convey the subtle pleasures of pleasure. There is an even simpler resolution to the issue, however. Judgemental people—and I include my former self in this—say that fishing is boring. Fishing is only boring if you're not catching any fish, and no decent angler is ever prepared to admit he is not catching any fish.

Anyway, what's so bad about boredom? *Langweilen ist die Grundstimmung des Philosophierens,* a Berlin U-Bahn ad used to say, showing various slumped or blankly staring commuters: *Boredom is the basic condition for philosophizing.* That is not to say that philosophers are boring (though that may well be true in some cases); rather, that boredom is the beginning of philosophy. Sometimes, in the deep folds of inactivity—say, while fishing without success—where thoughts are allowed to wander because there is nothing else for them to do, new vistas open up.

The fantasy was always the same. I would be watching television, usually sports, on the single channel that my non-cable ten-inch black-and-white television picked out of the airwaves around New Haven during some dark days in the late 1980s. I'd see him: the guy with the simple job. The guy with no worries. The guy who stood at the top of the giant slalom run in Kitzbuehl, wearing cool sunglasses and a toque, who told the skiers to wait for the Longines count-down to begin. Or the guy whose only job was to drill the front right wheel's lug nuts as fast as possible during a Formula One pit stop.

I would envy this guy, whoever he was. I longed for the utter simplicity of his task in life. This guy, I thought, *this* guy's got it made, just doing this one simple thing that makes up his professional identity. He doesn't hesitate or stress. It's got to be done well but, in the ambit of human achievement, it's perfectly balanced, just demanding or dangerous enough to keep him interested without calling for the high-percentile skill-set of the actual skier or driver. I had no idea what sort of life path or educational profile brought him to one of those positions, couldn't at all judge the relative distance from my own arc, but I wanted to be one of those guys, wanted very much to be him instead of who I was. And that was mainly because I was a guy sitting on a crummy little couch in a chilly one-bedroom apart-ment, watching sports instead of writing a doctoral disser-tation in philosophy.

Stop me if you've heard this one: graduate student is procrastinating, avoiding work, fantasizing about life else-where, or just, you know, life. Stop me, because then I won't have to go on and that would mean I could do something else instead of what I ought to be doing. I don't know if graduate school in the humanities is an especially acute site of procrastination—with one thing and another, I rather think it is—but I do know that a philosophy of procrastination cries out to be written, an examination of its peculiar phenomenology and ingeniously twisted logic. Its intricate mixture of self-justification and self-loathing. Its self-defeating spirals of defensible deferral. Its paralyzing pleasures and subtle pains . . .

And so on, sprawled there on the couch. This was a key moment of procrastination, in fact, because its essence lay not simply in avoiding what ought to be done, but in thinking of other things that could be done, even while not doing *them*. As all of its dedicated practitioners know, procrastination is far more creative than mere laziness, indeed is related only distantly to that passive affliction. Procrastination can be very active, though not in the way that the reform-minded surgeons of procrastination would have you believe.

The stasis at the heart of procrastination's sometimes frenzied displacement is most often driven by the idea that there is *too much to do,* the important task or tasks too big to tackle. After all, you can't write a four-hundred-page document in one go, any more than you can hit the proverbial five-run homer with one swing. Procrastination is linked at this conceptual juncture to its variform cousin, writer's block, at least in one virulent strain—namely, trying too hard such that you not only fail, but fail by not trying. (Of which more later.)

In the pitifully meagre literature on procrastination—meagre, that is, considering how much and how often procrastination structures human affairs—there is a lot of emphasis on the fact that procrastinators don't actually do *nothing*. They sort magazines or make shopping lists or, famously, sharpen pencils. And this displaced activity is where the reformer seeks to impose the otherwise misplaced use-values of the neglected task. Most of the writing on procrastination is thus far too solution-oriented or prevention-driven to be really deep in the sense we philosophers like; it wants to find ways to make problems go away rather than finding reasons why they can't. So writers advise the procrastination-afflicted that they should, instead of sharpening pencils (or when a sufficiency of pencils has been sharpened), make a list of the tasks they have to accomplish! Further, they ought to break the overwhelming task into manageable smaller ones and make a start that way! Lists are good here, lists make life more submissive to sense. A list is a tool for working with! You have a list in your hand, you start ticking off the items, and pretty soon you're making progress. The thousand-mile journey begins with one step!

But any true procrastinator knows this is nonsense. As an old *New Yorker* cartoon had it, the thousand-mile journey actually begins with the thought that a thousand miles is a hell of a long way. As for lists, the very thought of making them makes experienced procrastinators tired. The whole point of procrastination's displacement activity is not that it's active but that it's *displaced*. The whole point. Procrastinators are masters of inventive self-deception but they're also masters at seeing through, and so being unconvinced by, attempts at corrective self-deception. You can't fool a procrastinator into doing useful work just by displacing his displacement, dressing up avoidance as achievement. He's seen that one before. He practically invented that one.

Indeed, this Puritanical drive to save the dedicated procrastinator from his own flaws is revealed as no more than an imposition of external authority in the form of social approval, otherwise known as civilization. The English poet Edward Young called procrastination "the thief of time" in 1742 and most commentators since have been bent on bringing the miscreant to justice. But why? What's so great about time?

Procrastination visits all manner of people in all kinds of occupations, of course, but there are good reasons why writing is a prime location for it. There is a single large task with an unspecific deadline, which is to say, no deadline at all. The work is difficult and yet almost entirely devoid of impact on the outside world. There are few lively prospects of financial success, much anxiety about a slide into obscurity, and yet a dream of a cozy life somehow remains vivid enough that the only thing more difficult than finishing is walking away. Those who do walk away—or "pluck the leech," as we used to say—tend to have a hard time shaking off the experience.

The writer is engaged in a task of seeming importance, therefore, at least within the chosen tribe, which nevertheless feels at once pressing and pointless. The time frame for this task is just long enough to induce daily ennui without being general enough to succumb to the ease of daily effort. Contrast this with the task of staying fit, say, about which many people experience procrastinatory moments. Staying fit has no deadline. There may be a teleological notion of "getting in shape," but this is general enough to accept any effort as worthwhile—taking the stairs instead of the elevator—even while being sufficiently undefined as to be finally unrealizable. Finishing a book is a goal both strict and vague—a fatal conjunction.

Humans are, on the whole, more responsive to external constraints than internal ones, and every drill-sergeant knows the flimsy limits of the untrained superego. The basis of most training, indeed, whatever its end, is to effect internalization of external authority. Freud was probably right that this is the linchpin of all human societies. Absent a strong external pressure or a successfully imposed internal one, there are no incentives for doing anything that involves effort, pain, self-denial, or deferral of other pleasures. Or for doing anything at all. From this vantage, the unwritten book, like a capricious parent, realizes the worst possible combination when it comes to external authority—namely, long-term presence but short-term absence. It both infantilizes its subjects and demands a degree of mature self-discipline it cannot guarantee.

Thus the pressing need to avoid. Every avoided task has its associated rituals, but in writing these tend to be especially magical in quality, gesturing in hopeful sympathetic ways toward the actual unpursued task. I mean things such as going out of the room with the fervent hope that computer elves will, in your absence, assemble assorted notes and semi-random files into a finished book.

But such measures, while both inventive and psychically effective, don't really count as procrastination. They are too closely related to the task at hand, and might even eventually mutate somehow into its completion; or they might, as in Geoff Dyer's memoir-novel *Out of Sheer Rage,* desperately mutate one literary task (writing a biography of D.H.

Lawrence) into another literary task (writing a memoir-novel about writing a biography of D.H. Lawrence). That is too facile a move, since, as all writers know, the only thing easier than reading about writing is writing about it.

Genuine, or classical, procrastination must have less connection to the real job even while preserving some link, however tenuous, to its non-completion. That is, gardening *qua* gardening is not procrastination; only gardening as a way of not getting on with the dissertation is. This difference is subtle and often, like the one between Kierkegaard's knight of faith and the ordinary bourgeois citizen, invisible to the outside eye. Only I can know for sure that what I am doing is a way of not doing something else. And sometimes my self-deception demands that even *I* don't know, which makes things all the more interesting.

Which is why fishing, like all forms of contemplative leisure, is such an important activity: it is a way of doing something so that the thought of not doing other things *does not even arise!*

Procrastination's closest cousin, at least in mood, is boredom, though it remains importantly distinct. The psychoanalyst Adam Phillips has described boredom as "that state of suspended anticipation in which things are started and nothing begins, the mood of diffuse restlessness which contains that most absurd and paradoxical wish, the wish for a desire." Procrastination differs from boredom more subtly than it differs from laziness (i.e., active versus passive) because in procrastination, unlike in boredom, one's desires are engaged. Engaged, yes, but twisted. Procrastination is not boredom's paradoxical wish for a desire, but the perversion of a desire through self-deluded displacement. The procrastinator may be bored, I suppose, but it is more likely that he staves off the boredom he would otherwise feel during a period of inaction precisely by substituting another action, and its attendant desires, for the first one, whose completion he officially (and maybe even really) desires.

In fact, though, we all know it is more complicated than simple substitution, and accounts of procrastination that emphasize bare intentionality—and hence culpability—get the matter badly wrong. In structure, procrastination's closest relative is actually *addiction,* and that is one reason why the symptoms of acquisitiveness and insatiability so often visit the smitten angler, that master of procrastination.

As the philosopher Harry Frankfurt has argued, the best way to understand the addict (following, among other things, Plato's analysis of *akrasia,* or weakness of the will) is that he has first-order desire which, at the second order, he does not desire: he wants the drug (or whatever) but does not want to want it. Thus use of the drug entails both pleasure (first-order desire satisfied) and shame (second-order desire flouted). This further explains why the addict may be considered to be, in a sense, at war with himself—and so at least potentially open to therapeutic intervention at the margin between the first and second order.

Most of us are also familiar with a different version of desire conflict, namely, having second-order desires for first-order desires we don't have. Indeed, this is what we usually mean by weakness of the will in common parlance: I want to want to do the right thing, I just don't want to do it. There is also the possible case of a willing addict, when first- and second-order desires for a drug line up. Such people are usually beyond helping, and will fish until dark, spend all their money on new tackle they don't need, and forget to call—or sometimes go—home.

Procrastination looks like simple weakness of the will but it retains potent addictive qualities as well. The pleasure of creatively putting things off is real, if often indefensible: it's a clear head rush, at once comforting and wickedly exhilarating, like the first sip of a cold gin martini. It casts doubt and failure into a costless future. Procrastination is "the art of keeping up with yesterday," Don Marquis has Archy tell Mehitabel, but the Latin roots of the word actually suggest a casting forward of tasks into tomorrow—*pro-crastinare*. In *On the Road,* Jack Kerouac dwells lovingly on the low-key attitude of the Mexican migrant workers he encountered in California, who, he said, made *mañana* sound like the most beautiful word in any language. Procrastination can look anxious, even harried—*mañanamania*—but it is more properly languorous, droopy, beautiful. If the putting off is done by, say, making a few notes or entertaining a few thoughts about the larger project, its satisfaction is genuine. Still better is the simple comforting thought of how well, how much more happily and certainly, you will approach the task tomorrow, the sense of purpose and rightness you will enjoy as you sit down to write or compose or telephone . . . tomorrow.

The shame of procrastination is almost wholly unnecessary when viewed from the proper perspective. But procrastination's peculiar spiral of shame has its own fascination to the analyst. Take a common kind of procrastination: failing to return a phone call to a friend.

Over the course of maybe forty-eight hours, depending on the closeness of the friendship or association, this is no failure at all. Then, at a certain point, the phone call moves from not-yet-returned status to the officially unreturned category. At this point, the issue of the call's non-return is superadded to whatever else the call entailed. Now, you have an extended disincentive for calling, which can only grow as time passes: the longer you have not called, the more your not-calling is the subject of any possible call. Then, at another precise but varying point, the issue of the call is too big to face and the possibility of actually making it lowers to nil. Now you reason that it is almost better *not* to call, because calling is so fraught with potential bad feeling. You have passed a point of no return. The call was never a painful task, one avoided because unpleasant; it just became an avoided task, and then an inconceivable one, by the inexorable passage of time.

The spiral also works with letters and e-mails and other forms of personal communication. This is of course why so-called organized people try to return calls and e-mails as immediately as possible, often out of fear. Sensitive souls can find the shame-spiral terrifying because it happens so often and so inevitably. It is the procrastinatory equivalent of the death-spin that claims the lives of small-craft pilots who become disoriented in bad weather or darkness and, not trusting their instruments, actually steer into the downward loops that will eventually encompass their ruin. It is also, in its way, related to the information-action paralysis that sometimes afflicts airline check-in personnel or line cooks when confronted by sudden unmanageable volumes of work.

In these service occupations, there is a naive (because often counter-demonstrated) assumption that the flow of tasks—customers, orders—will more or less self-regulate. During calm or only slightly busy times, this is so. But when there is a sudden spike in volume, the assumption is overturned with disastrous results. Without a reliable principle of triage, each equally important and demanding customer or food order piles in right behind the other. The worker tries to self-regulate, ranking the incoming tasks to deal with them more efficiently, but this ranking is itself a new task that leaches time away from the primary task. Soon, lacking the necessary scheme of external regulation, an overload point is reached and there is no principled way of retreating from it. The system of action, predicated on steady-but-staggered flow rather than rank-ordered flow, breaks down. Result: task gridlock. The check-in gate is a scene of chaos; the cook is in the weeds. Sean tells a particularly harrowing story of just standing in his kitchen at work, staring at orders piling in from the wait staff, others hopelessly backed up, people yelling, the ranges full, and simply *not knowing what to do.*

Kitchen shell-shock. He would, it is fair to say, rather have been fishing.

You might be thinking, so what? You might be thinking of some calls you should be returning right now. You might be thinking a lot of things that aren't getting any work done. But there is a deeper lesson still waiting for us, always waiting, and it is what I've been meaning to get to, standing there in the boat and thinking, doing something that is, by definition, not useful, not a task, and therefore easy enough to get to.

Suppose I am meant to be writing a book. Since this is my job, or anyway one key aspect of it, writing isn't just any old thing I might or might not do, like gardening or staying fit. It counts as an important, even essential, task within the highly artificial and contingent universe of meaning out of which I have constructed my identity. I am a writer of books, and therefore must continue to write books in order to maintain the coherence of that identity, vulnerable as it is through the passage of time. At a certain point, hard to define but inevitable, if I have written no further books, I slip, like an unreturned telephone call, from the status of deliberate writer into the status of former writer. This shift is distinct from but oddly related to the familiar law, first noticed by Auden, which dictates that all writers under forty are "young" while all writers over forty are "failing to fulfill their promise."

Suppose further that I am thirty-nine years old at the time I am thinking this, casting my line. Suppose I am under contract to write a book. Having written a few books already, there is some lively expectation that I will not only write this new book but deliver its manuscript in a timely fashion, *hitting* the deadline, as we like to say, aggressively, as if printing out a big pile of manuscript pages were comparable to an NBA-championship slam dunk or act of military ordnance delivery.

But suppose I am having some trouble. The book is not getting written. The pile of manuscript pages is not rising from the desktop with reliable speed, and the file labelled "Chapter One" is filled with notes but not sentences. Having never suffered from it before, I wonder if this constitutes writer's block. But I have no trouble writing, I just have trouble writing the book. Or rather, I have no trouble *not* writing the book. Some of the writing I'm doing in the meantime is personal, some professional. I write newspaper columns and essays and reference letters. I even get paid for some of these. But the book . . . the book lies unwritten, days on end. Ironically, if that's what I mean, one of its tentative titles is *Losing Your Way*. It purports to be a meditation on the city as a metaphor for human existence, the illuminating combination of chaos and order in street grids and transactions and desire-manipulation. It's about reading the dreams of walking in the city.

In graduate school I solved all instances of couch-potato stall with a time-tested manoeuvre. I used to get up every morning at eight o'clock and, without glancing at a newspaper or talking to anyone else, walk into the kitchen to put the kettle on. On the way past the boxy little Macintosh on my desk, I would flip the power switch and then listen for the *hum* of its arising consciousness. Coffee in hand, I would sit down and start writing. A thousand words or so—the professional writer's mantra—and I'd call it a day. After that point, more effort usually yielded fewer results, so there was no point going on. I would run, eat a late lunch, and then teach or hang out, depending which day it was. Luckily, I had some excellent baseline training to fall back on: my childhood spent in a family headed by a military man married to a woman (an otherwise loving mother) who came from a family where sleeping in was considered morally repugnant. I did the Macintosh manoeuvre regularly for days and weeks together, a clockwork process of grinding up my chosen topic by ignoring potential evasions or expansions, head down, and eventually produced the document that secured my entry into the impossible profession of philosophy.

Fine. Better than fine, really, since this monkish morning ritual continued to work for books, when I thought I had something to say and knew how to say it. Like everyone else who writes books, I tried always (after Graham Greene's advice) to finish a day's work with the lead sentence of a new paragraph, so I could spring from my bed with a glad heart and begin pounding away at the keys again. I avoided the temptation to read over what I had written in a given day and simply pressed on. I didn't spend a lot of time discussing the subject with anyone else, heeding the solid axiom that when you're talking you're not writing. These and other tricks of the trade served me well in avoiding the avoidance of procrastination. But, at a certain point—I mean now—they did so no longer.

It seems to me there are two forms of writer's block that are rational and therefore to be actively feared. (There may of course be other, irrational forms posing their own dangers.) One is the weary blankness that results from seeing the contours of your book's subject too clearly, knowing too far in advance exactly what you need to say. Writing coaches often say a detailed outline is the surest way to defeat procrastination, but the hidden danger is that such an outline instead defeats the fun of writing, reducing the project to a mechanical task devoid of interest, even, or especially, for the author. Writing that was no fun for the writer confesses itself pretty quickly. Nobody wants to read it, and nobody sane wants to write it. As a writer you look at the outline, the whole thing mapped and sketched, and a great heaviness lowers onto your shoulders. Now the book is like laundry or an income-tax return. You think, *Surely, in an advanced service economy like this one, there is someone I can pay to do this for me while I go fishing?*

The other kind of block is deeper. Instead of coming attached to boredom, as above, it comes attached to boredom's own nasty near-relation, depression. And here procrastination is revealed as merely the surface manifestation of a more profound malaise, something on the order of Bartleby's refusal to scribe or what Geoff Dyer calls, more simply, *despair*.

I said that procrastination most often arises from a sense that there is too much to do, and hence no single aspect of the to-do worth doing. On that level, it is a bit like going to a store and seeing lots of things you might buy but no single thing you feel motivated to buy. But underneath this rather antic form of action-as-inaction is the much more unsettling question whether anything at all is worth doing.

Once you start not-doing one big project, in other words, it's an open question whether you should maybe not-do a bunch of others. The Stoic philosopher Epictetus: "Anything worth putting off is worth abandoning altogether." Indeed. Pretty soon you're not only not getting up and turning on the computer right away, you're not getting up at all. "Give up one thing and you're immediately obliged to do something else," Dyer writes of the procrastinatory end-game. "The only way to give up totally is to kill yourself but that one act requires an assertion of will equal to the total amount that would be expended in the rest of a normal lifetime." And so that is not worth doing, either, any more than this or that smaller thing. Checkmate.

That is at once true and terribly unhelpful. Life is often a matter of just getting on with things because the alternative is too terrible to countenance. This is procrastination's bleak underlying message. And the brave thinker's job is to acknowledge that danger frankly and yet make that countenance his or her own: to flee toward rather than away from the threat. At every moment, big-time stalls or, alternatively, excessive self-medication to deal with our dismay over being so stalled (as David Hume and AA alike sagely warn) threaten to get the better of us.

Once again, I cannot be certain philosophy is particularly afflicted by the terminal form of procrastination, what we might agree to call *the not-doing of everything*, but I suspect it may be so. When it comes to wondering why, philosophy is obviously a high-risk activity. Consider the possibilities. In many cases, philosophical subjects sail close to the limits of the sayable, attempting to articulate, for instance, the conditions of possibility of any form of knowledge or the final dynamic nature of reality. Philosophy is thus a form of activity always on the verge of asking why any activity has point! Even to accept the confines of propositions is, at this point, the act of someone gripped by either arrogance or folly. It was no joke when Wittgenstein, attempting to join logic and language, concluded his *Tractatus Logico-Philosophicus* with the claim (warning? injunction?) that what we cannot speak of, we must pass over in silence.

In the great pro-sports tradition, Wittgenstein made a comeback from this early impasse, offered up a new philosophy of language, and generally created a thriving academic industry of commentary on and secondary interpretation of his works. Good for him. Still, he spent his last days in a canvas deck chair in his rooms at King's College, Cambridge, going quietly mad, racked by thoughts of suicide. After hours of hard thought, he might scribble a remark in a notebook, retire for bed, and then rise to crumple the previous day's work. As he confessed in the preface to his *Philosophical Investigations,* this stringency had its costs: "I should have liked to produce a good book," Wittgenstein says there. "This has not come about, but the time is past in which I could improve it." Yes, because that time is always past. To submit to publication is necessarily to embrace the futility of accepting that you cannot say what you mean to say, and so to embrace the futility of even attempting to do so.

This devil's bargain, ever a feature of committing thought to the page, or really of doing anything at all rather than nothing, calls forth different kinds of reaction in different people. It is, in its quietly desperate way, a test of character. It is no wonder so many scholars hie themselves off to the recondite and abstruse regions of their subject, places where small-bore precision and recondite distinctions carry the day. Here, disdaining anything too deep or tongue-tying, it is easy to remain distracted and so churn out the journal articles of interest only to those wielding the same precise distinctions.

On the other hand, trying to write something more lasting and more profound is bound to invite Seneca's cold reminder that the esteem of future generations is no more valuable than that of the present one. All esteem—past, present, or future—is capricious and devoid of any meaning beyond popularity. We often invoke the supposedly illuminating lesson of the genius who went uncelebrated in his own day, or, conversely, the dismal morality tale of the man once beyond fame who now reclines in obscurity. But really both arcs are equally meaningless. They rest upon a fallacious premise—namely, that our regard is inherently superior to any before or since.

In any event, to recall another wry Greek maxim, in neither case is the subject around to enjoy or suffer the judgement. Would Seneca like to know that he is still invoked thousands of years after his demise? Sure, but he can't and therefore doesn't. Tough luck is, finally, the only kind there is.

By the time you reach this point in the argument, if it's an argument, standing there casting your line instead of working, procrastination begins to look not only forgivable but eminently reasonable. Indeed, it is often needlessly concerned with its relationship to the main, avoided task, which has no inherent justification and therefore claims no place, let alone the top one, on any to-do list. Procrastination thus becomes the possible prelude to a principled idleness. You think, *I must learn to stop worrying about not doing things and simply enjoy the not-doing of everything.* Not leisure for the sake of culture or recreation, in other words, but leisure for the sake of leisure. Wise men from Solon in the ancient world to the Enlightenment editors of *The Idler* and *Lounger* to modernism's favourite rebel, Oscar Wilde, thought this was the right, the only, answer when it came to the issue of doing anything at all. Idleness is the one form of life that solves the problem of which procrastination is the symptom. Let's go fishing!

It is, of course, far harder to be idle than we often think. Finding meaningful recreation is not child's play, despite what you may have heard. The playboy-novelist Ian Fleming was once credited by one of his friends with having "a great talent for organized leisure," which is a more considerable compliment, and a rarer quality, than it sounds. The great task of tasklessness is staving off boredom or ennui, the weariness of having nothing particular to do, for when you can do anything, you can just as easily do nothing. Idleness can then become, bizarrely, a demanding full-time occupation, and so may seem to court self-defeat: avoiding avoidance by inverting the not-yet logic of procrastination, it succumbs to dominant use-values anyway.

Work and its rhythms are hard to avoid in human affairs, of course, since most of us derive pleasure not just from achievement but from its implicit contrast with other forms of time-spending. We want things to look forward to, structuring pleasant goals that offset routine and drudgery. One reason people find breakups (and, still more, close deaths) so unsettling and depressing is that they lose, at a stroke, a person with whom they have become used to planning their diversions, whatever those may be. A future is lost, and so a sense of wholeness or identity, however flimsy and variable. "I just don't know what to do with myself" gets it about half right; the other half is "I just don't know what to think of myself." Looking-forward-to is a bargain with the future, a healthy and vibrant one in contrast to procrastination's anxious one. Because of this, the dedicated idler is thus always in danger of becoming just another worker—and possibly worse off than other workers, since what does he have to look forward to, after all, when no pleasure ever needs to be deferred?

Accomplished idlers are familiar with these twinned dangers and tend to navigate their shoals instinctively, not working too hard at not-working and yet inventing artificial goals and imaginary (but diverting) obstacles to pleasure. And indeed, angling has long been one of their favourite pastimes—elegant, absorbing, and time-consuming without ever succumbing to mere use-value and hence becoming work. Anglers are connoisseurs of the world of pleasure, finding their rhythms there, but there is always the danger that we begin to take it too seriously, to make this calmest of recreations a form of competitive engagement hostile to the ends of recreation.

Which is all very interesting, but I'm just avoiding the real subject.

So here I am, trying to fish, trying to let go and not-write a book instead of trying and failing to write it. It happened that I moved to New York for a while just after I signed the contract for the book, the thought (and word) being that I would work hard on the book while there. This seemed reasonable, not least because the book, titled, as you may recall, *Losing Your Way,* was concerned in part with the urban experience, in particular the possibilities of walking in the city as a vehicle for more general ideas about desire, transaction, work, and idleness.

The trouble, as I soon realized, was that, as so many more have discovered before me, it's not easy to work in so head-turning a place. To the usual possible distractions—reading just one more book, wading through the papers, checking out websites—were added the beckoning temptations of simply walking the streets. I wanted to write but wanted more to do what I was supposedly writing about.

So for hours and hours, block upon block, I walked the streets of Manhattan. I walked uptown to Central Park, downtown to Battery Park. I walked across the Brooklyn Bridge and back, daytime and nighttime, always stopping in the open middle to admire the beautiful, fractured skyline of my adopted island home. I stopped to lounge in Madison Square or Bryant Park, bought deli sandwiches and kept walking, fuelled by strong coffee and a sense of possibility. I saw lots of remarkable and weird things, and felt, as so many have, the joys of anonymity, New York's underrated gift. ("To no other metropolis on earth," Kenneth Tynan said, "do I return more certain that I have not been missed.")

I noted details of type design in signs and logos, picked out architectural details, heard the voices of Lewis Mumford and Jane Jacobs in my head, looked through eyes conditioned by Evans and Abbott and Bourke-White. I walked over the much-trodden sidewalks, adding my idiosyncratic trails to the palimpsest of the world, thinking and talking to myself all the while.

But not writing. "Only thoughts that come from *walking* have any value," said Nietzsche, like most men of his era and nationality a great hiker around the mountain spa towns of Europe. And yet, at some point he had to sit down somewhere and write that, putting in the hours after the hours, finding the thought again and confining it—albeit nicely, appositely, as so often with him—in the prison of language. Aristotle's vision of peripatetic philosophy is all very well, an enjoyable way to pass the time, but it doesn't get the books written, or the thoughts clarified. Only actual writing—the active thinking of the seated—can do that. Even Izaak Walton had to stop fishing in order to write about fishing.

And yet, and yet. Does writing solve or only defer the issue? Who will read what we write? How many people, and to what purpose? At what point—achieving what volume of sales—is a book a success? Or, more subtly, how many minds does one have to change to justify the imposition of having tried to do so? Do we spend enough time considering how rude it is, really, how unseemly and arrogant, to foist another book on the world? At what point does not writing become, justifiably, not-writing?

And so walking, walking, more walking. Walking, thinking, and looking up. Walking, thinking, and losing my way. Casting and reeling, casting and reeling, thinking. And sooner or later, somewhere in there, I thought, like so many before me, that I had to stop putting life off for later, had to sit down. Because that's what I've been meaning to do.

Anyway, you can't fish for trout in the winter.

I was never once bored on the water, not even in the long meditative silences during which we gazed mutely at the bobbing DayGlo markers on the sun-dappled water or stood in the heavy current and traced a dry fly's slow movement across a pool. Hours pass without a sense of duration; time seems to fall through itself into a different state, what is sometimes called "flow" but is really a complete absence of that usual sense of things as strung along. Fishing and writing are the only things I know where one can exert a concentration that almost annihilates the sense of self, so that the passage of hours is only registered after the fact, when I look up and realize my neck is tense, my eyes sore, and I am ravenous because I forgot to eat.

Anyway, there was always plenty of action to interrupt the reflective clearings. We were very lucky, or very smart, or some magic combination thereof, which is probably the thing that makes all human endeavours compelling. We tried always just to fish, to fish not as a way of avoiding something else. Fishing as an end in itself. Sometimes, often enough, we managed it.

We must grow out of the youthful temptation to make fishing a competition, Grey advises. It is childish and crude to see your fellow Brothers of the Angle as opponents in a territorial game, the way you might regard the rugby players from another school. Of course, this wisdom typically arrives just about the time that one's athletic abilities are beginning to fade from full flower. It may be leisure, but angling is a complicated business and no man alive will deny the competitiveness, the striving for success, that colours every moment of this most contemplative form of not doing other things. There is a scene in *A River Runs Through It* where the father, watching his older son cast for trout, grabs a rock and heaves it into the stream right where the young man has just laid down his fly. They laugh, and it is the laughter of men.

So, yeah, we all know it's not supposed to be about the numbers or the weight, it's not a contest, and Steve doesn't actually *suck* at trout fishing, but . . . well, who cares. Over the three days of the first Weekend, I caught and released twenty-five rainbows. The next time out, over two days, I caught thirty-four. I kept two of that last haul for breakfast, lightly breaded and fried in butter, with scrambled eggs, bacon, toast, and coffee.

"You know, Mark," Fred said to me at one point that year, "not many people can keep up with me when it comes to fishing."

I'll take that.

Day after tomorrow I have to return to New York, and I will exchange stream for street, country for city, with my book still unwritten and, as the man says, no sense of having been missed—but I'll take that.

9

Comfort

"[We] have the paradox . . . of what might be called democratic solipsism, each of us exclusive total ruler of the world that depends on our mind for existence . . . and none of us able to discernibly exist except as subject of others' consciousness."

—E.L. Doctorow, *City of God*

I stood in the boat and cast. Cast and reeled, cast and reeled. Looking for success, sometimes finding it. Looking to strike, sometimes doing so. Trial and error. Conjecture and refutation.

Is it comfort we seek, on the water? A sense of connection with a larger meaning? Or just respite from having to think too hard or too directly? Just a pocket of near-emptiness where the time is not measured, does not press, and so passes without anxiety? Something like that, maybe.

The largeness of the universe mocks human ambition as surely now as it did in Walton's day, the worldly cares of men reduced to so much chatter, distraction, worry. And even our real achievements are mocked by scalar comparisons: a book or a child or a prize no proof against the battering siege of wrackful days, no justification for the time spent in its genesis. Why work? Why create? Why breed? The drops from the taut flyline into the vast cold lake are no less significant than our works and woes, the things we gather up near ourselves for warmth when the world offers none. We are tossed on currents of force that are indifferent to us, our consciousness made functionally redundant in a field of genetic and social transfer, the vast mute grid of adaptation. Genes, as Richard Dawkins famously said, are *selfish;* they have their own ends of survival to pursue, and our sense of ourselves, our fragile existence as individuals, is just a vehicle they exploit. Take a long enough (or reductive enough) view of evolution through natural selection and no life, however grand and impressive, is really world-historical. Only life itself, the struggle to adapt and survive, is that.

If God does not exist, can we ever find comfort? If there is no direction or grand plan—no meta-narrative that is not blind to our strivings—can we ever find ourselves at home here? Every visit is temporary. Is every visit also fated to be pointless? Alone as we are, there is one thing—maybe the only thing—that is proof against even the most overwhelming sense of absorption. Uniqueness, like a will in probate law, proves itself. You are not much; neither am I. And though we hope the things or people or culture we create may outlive us in our fragile, vulnerable meat-cage bodies, they are likewise cosmically flimsy: they do not last in any scale of deep time that we can imagine.

But let it be said, for better or worse—and surely it is always a mixture of both—that there is nothing else quite like us, no story exactly the same as yours or mine. To be sure, this is small solace, and always fleeting like the rise of the trout you long for, but it is real. As real as anything ever gets. On good days, it is just exactly as much as we need.

But here's the tricky thing: entry into some walks of life often coincides with the onset of ineradicable anxiety about whether you belong there. Marriage, parenthood, professional commitment. Maybe adulthood itself. What is it, anyway, to finish growing up? No amount of surface contentment can obliterate that undertone of misgiving; indeed, as the days wind their way on, full of activity and challenge and meals to share, the axis may tilt and certain things, formerly considered stable, might simply fall off the world. Lorrie Moore says we enter that stage of life, somewhere between twenty-five and thirty-eight, that is properly called *stupidity*. I read that a year ago and realized, not without amusement, that these were pretty much the years of my marriage.

That is not at all fair, really, just as the future is never all bleak. There is success, not small; there is happiness that is genuine, also not small. And you may, if you are lucky, bracket for long stretches the feeling that all this might not make too much sense, that something is amiss, that your picture of (as it might be) flickering outdoor candles and smiling faces, with its soft sound of songbook jazz and affection, is somehow false, distorted. You will forget, or put aside, the feelings of unease, shouldering a path some way into the world.

The forgetting will not last forever, because that kind of worldly path, the path of success and forgetting, is not meant to last. It is enough to get you some way along the harder road of just living. But unless you are prematurely old, you can't know how shocking, how thoroughgoing, will be the onset of what a Jane Smiley narrator calls "the age of grief," the time, say in the middle thirties or thereabouts, where everything, including happiness itself, begins to make you sad. "It is not only that we know love ends, children are stolen, parents die feeling that their lives have been meaningless," the character reflects. "It is more that the barriers between the circumstances of oneself and the rest of the world have broken down, after all." Nothing holds death at bay forever, not even stupidity.

Well, yes. You are, thank God, still young enough to tamp down that creeping feeling of mortal unease without denying it, to imagine briefly more goals to pursue, more achievements to crave, to turn the music up a little higher and pour one more glass and think of other things entirely. I said before that philosophy has been called the art of learning how to die. In more modern terms, we might call it the practice of *imaginary deathbed psychodrama:* forcing a confrontation with mortality in a controlled environment, the laboratory of reflection—like art, a cathartic opportunity under conditions of relative safety. A full-time concern, but not a full-time possibility. "I am at first affrighted and confounded with that forlorn solitude in which I am placed by my philosophy," David Hume wrote, "and fancy myself some uncouth monster, utterly abandoned and disconsolate. Fain would I run into the crowd for shelter and warmth." But, he added, though flight was ever a temptation, the reality was more homely: sometimes it's enough to play backgammon or have a drink. "Be a philosopher," Hume advised. "But in your philosophizing, be also a man."

You are wise enough to catch that deep thought, and then release it. After all, you can't be expected to think hard all the time. If nothing else, at some point, no matter how timeless and mortal your waterside reflections, you must think about making dinner.

Fishing teaches us that the problems of ethics begin as problems in epistemology, the apparently unbridgeable distance between each of us alone. "[W]e who fish are a savage race," says Morley Roberts. "Our philosophy is a kind of solipsism. When I fish I am the universe. There is none but me. . . . A true fisherman cannot bear another human within a mile of him, unless he has something noble to show."

And therein lies the issue, since we both want to be alone and need sometimes to share our noble victories. The basic issue of all ethical reflection is the difficulty of living with others—that they cannot be evaded, even on the water. We need them. At some point, we all must return to the society from which fishing, like all genuine recreations, is both a respite and a reflection. "A fisherman is not properly a social animal," Roberts adds, and that is so. But sometimes the man who fishes must be. Though we might like to, we cannot stay on the river forever.

This tension runs so strongly through reflection on angling as to constitute its major theme, and no one can be surprised thereby; it is, we might say, the basic dialectic of solitude and society from which all the others proceed: beauty and utility, reflection and action, co-operation and competition. Viscount Grey reminds us—and he was, we should remember, Foreign Secretary of Great Britain at the time—that we must always make the return journey from the countryside chalkstream to the streets of London, the place where, in addition to all life's joys, we find too the wickedness of our shared civic life. This opposition, which can be found in both ancient and modern versions, stands in marked contrast to Medieval and Renaissance ideas that the city is the site of safety and justice, and the countryside where rape and robbery abound; such is the basis, for example, of the contrasting allegories of Justice and Injustice executed by Giotto in Padua's Arena Chapel.

Giotto or no Giotto, the salubrity of country air is a standard preoccupation of pastoral poetry from Juvenal to

Johnson, and fishing is for many of us the modern-day pastoral. Dr. Johnson was notoriously hard on fishing, but his ungenerous assessment must surely proceed from ignorance. "Fly fishing may be a very pleasant amusement," he said, "but angling or float fishing I can only compare to a stick and a string, with a worm on one end and a fool on the other." He is on surer ground in his great poem about London, metaphor for cities and civilizations everywhere: "Here malice, rapine, accident, conspire / And now a rabble rages, now a fire . . ." Indeed. And yet we must return there from our lakes and streams, even from the "purer air" we "breathe in distant fields." The question: "For who would leave, unbrib'd, Hibernia's land / Or change the rocks of Scotland for the Strand?" The answer: Johnson for one; also Boswell, his Scottish tagalong. Here, London and Hibernia are no more real places than the choice between them is a genuine one. Sooner or later, all recreations give way to the reality of coexistence; we must unfix the rod, wind the reel a final time, and leave clear mountain air for the conspiring city, the warm breath of others.

Then what? How is it possible for me, for this consciousness I call myself, to bridge the gap between what I experience directly and what I presume (but can only presume) is the experience of another? My consciousness cannot exceed its own limits and it cannot encompass itself;

it is like a flashlight whose beam, no matter how bright, cannot illuminate its own source. And so it is, finally, impossible for me to be conscious of your consciousness. I am only aware of my own experience of what I call you, another conscious person. This is not so much a gap to be bridged, then, as it is an apparently insuperable problem in possibility. When I reflect on what I actually know, I know you only as a feature of my own experience. The same, of course, is true for you; thus the basis of Doctorow's "democratic" solipsism. We're all in this together—together and alone.

This presumption of shared aloneness is thin but necessary, and it is the basis for all ethical obligations of care and respect. There is a necessary reciprocity of perspectives among consciousnesses, a complex convergence of (what we choose to call) shared experiences. There are numerous vehicles for this kind of convergence, the most important of which is language. Other vehicles—institutions and rules and social infrastructures of all kinds—are themselves discursive achievements, through and through.

Though the feelings of another person are inaccessible to us, a shared language means we can nevertheless be moved by the signs and descriptions and evidence of those feelings. We cannot feel anyone else's pain, but we *can* be pained at the thought of pain in another. Emotional connection, and the moral imagination that makes it possible, is an indispensable move in the ethical game. For I will not be moved to treat you with respect and dignity if I do not already view you as a significant entity—that is, as an entity who I presume feels the same kinds of things I feel. Basic feelings like pain and pleasure, hunger and cold—but also more complex experiences like triumph and humiliation, shame and anger.

There are risks as well as rewards here, as we all know. Accepting the limits and obligations of our democratic solipsism can be painful: the pain of loss, the pain of failure, the pain of time itself—the way the past impinges on the present, the way the shadow of the future falls over our attempts to act well, to be ethical. Each of us who claims to be conscious bears a burden of responsibility that is vast and growing: to all other conscious entities, to vulnerable creatures and ecosystems, even to ideas and values that exist only in their own exercise. Reflecting on the nature of the ethical society is not just philosophically challenging; it is also emotionally trying. Like the theatre-goers described centuries ago by Aristotle, we put ourselves in a fragile, volatile state whenever we reflect on the nature of our obligations.

We do not—cannot—love every other conscious being. But we can and must look to love's lessons for insight into the basic nature of all obligation. Love is the limit case of emotional attachment, the test of our deepest attachments and vulnerabilities. Love is, in turn, often most deeply felt, most poignant, in its loss. Those are the stakes, after all, when we venture into it. And so, as a beginning (but only a beginning) to the larger, ongoing, indeed infinite task of making connections and seeking the good—the human task of building care and justice—I offer the following moments of painful reflection. They start by enjoining forgetfulness but end with remembrance and the beginning of another episode in the strange, joyful, interrupted journey that is my conscious life—what we choose to call, in this particular shared language, *a new day*.

When that new day dawns, we shall look out the cabin window. And if the rain has held off, and the light is good, and the air is clear, we will load the gear, get in the boat or pull on the hip waders, and go hunting for trout.

Sean and I married sisters, Lorraine and Gail. First Sean and Lorraine got divorced, then Gail and I did. Sean met Lorraine, the older sister by a few years, at our wedding fifteen years ago. The two of them stayed together for a few years; we stayed together for a few years after that. Lorraine and Gail, the two Donaldson girls, from Edinburgh. Well,

Stirling really. One small, one less so; one intellectual, the other less so; both dark and pretty, with an almost identical crooked tooth in their National Health Service smiles.

People can be separated into two categories: (1) those who think two brothers marrying two sisters is *cute, fun,* or *wonderful;* (2) those who see the resulting array of cross-hatched loyalties, strained family gatherings, and persistent unspoken rivalries for the minefield it is.

Kingsley Amis, in a voice belonging to one of his cranky middle-aged characters, says "divorce is one of the most violent things we know." True. Also sad and shocking and, to use a misused word for once in its proper sense, shameful.

Sample questions from your friends in the months, then years, after your separation become not just a temporary aberration or logistical manoeuvre but a permanent reality: Are you ever going to get married again? Don't you think you should settle down? What did you expect, dating someone ten years younger than you?

Well, exactly. You know the type. Or, if you don't, you pretty soon will. Her thousand-yard stare when the bill arrives. Flirting with other guys at the bar. Emotional terrorism as a substitute for personality. Astonishing feats of double-standard logic. Also, pretty as hell, funny, living in New York. Tom Wolfe: "New York is great for sex. But you have to leave New York to fall in love."

So you do. But out here on the lake, the mind free to wander, your sad younger brother a rod's length away, marriage and its aftermath creeps back into mind whether you like it or not. The persistence of grief, even when everything else fades.

Forget for a moment, if you can, the fact that it comes upon you without warning. On a train. Late at night, looking out the window. Standing waist-deep in the cold current of a stream.

Or when you are just washing the dishes, and suddenly collapse under the sandbag weight of it. Bent over the sink and the scattered archaeological remains of your backlogged solitary meals: plates used a few times over, now messy palettes of meat-juice earth tones and sticky-vegetable texture; knives smeared with hardened peanut butter or the intricate craquelure of old cream cheese; the red-wash mineral deposits of the wineglasses. The tears roll off your downturned nose and plop into the soapy, greasy water.

And you think: gone.

If you're like most people, there may be a tendency to wallow in your grief. "Some men, like bats or owls, have better eyes for the darkness than for the light," said Dickens. And indeed it is easy to see the shadows of life now, to seek them out. But it is more complicated than mere disposition (the eyes you have) or even brain chemistry (the serotonin levels you register). You find that grief is stealthy. It works by ambush: a song, a sight, a sound. The crush of feeling, once started, does not want to abate.

And so you spiral down. The past is gone; it won't come back. That, after all, is what the past does—that's how it works. That scene of your comfort will not return. You have forever lost that moment of happiness. Real or imagined, it doesn't matter. For surely (you reason) that comfort was in reality more complicated than it seems in retrospect, scored with irritation and boredom and trivial worries about getting the bus back or having enough money to pay for lunch. Yes. And yet, it just doesn't matter much because—well, because she is gone. Or because they are dead. Or because he is right now making moments with another, not you. That's what has happened. And you can't change any of it.

But here is the part you wonder at and maybe frown over. It feels good, in its own twisted way, to think these thoughts and have these wrenching feelings—to have the tears leak out of you even as you try, childishly, to push them back in. Yes, it feels oddly good, and this is something you find hard to defend rationally but nevertheless appreciate as also part of your humanness, your need for connection, your sense of shared vulnerability. The pain is real yet exquisite, the longing sharp and unwelcome, yet also, like all longing, stimulating and . . . wise. Admit it: somehow, giving way to mourning is a pleasure. You know this is true.

This is not masochism, though your friends and your therapist may want to argue. It is wallowing, and that is something else. Schopenhauer, that great pessimist, the connoisseur of all things boring and depressing, saw this very clearly. Pain, he said, is always also pleasure, and the perverse pleasure of mourning is one of the most interesting we know. If nothing else, it gives us a role to inhabit, a space of emergent meaning, a way of being in the world when the world seems—when the world is—drained of colour. It teaches us about the web of connection we have no choice but to inhabit, for reward and risk alike.

It can also, for the record, lead to art. The problem is, it doesn't have to; worse than that, it can lead to bad art just as easily as good. This is a risk for everybody. Put your pencils away. Avoid the keyboard. Mourning becomes Electra, but it doesn't become most of us: we simply don't have the talent.

Still, sometimes there is great art in mourning, and not all of it indulgent. Donne famously forbade it in his "Valediction" of 1633:

Our two souls therefore, which are one,
        Though I must go, endure not yet
A breach, but an expansion,
        Like gold to aery thinness beat.

If they be two, they are two so
        As stiff compasses are two,
The soul the fixed foot, makes no show
        To move, but doth, if th'other do.

And though it in the centre sit,
        Yet when the other far doth roam,
It leans, and hearkens after it,
        And grows erect, as that comes home.

So lovely and so sexy, in the oblique fashion that Donne, a man of much joy and grief both, practised with such easy geometrical skill. But the poem is, like so many poems about love, also false. Because if the two shall *never* meet again, then no matter how supple the airy thinness of beaten gold that binds them, it will not sustain the connection. The connection is severed—by misfortune, by time, by death, by things that are simply no longer what they were.

This final separation will always happen, sooner or later. Not because the love was false or mundane ("sublunary"

Donne calls the lesser kind, implying the transcendence of his own), or even because we all die (though that is part of it, see below), but rather because the other soul in question, the one that is lost, *isn't* the one belonging to the other person, the lost loved one.

It is, instead, the one belonging to the other *you,* the one who was there before but is, can be, there no longer. The lover you were when love was young, or just when it was alive. The one who tasted joy, like champagne, for the very first time. That is the hardest part: the lost loved one is not dead; you are. That version of yourself is done, over, and you can't get it back. You think you can, but you can't. And that, unfortunately, is once more the point.

Freud: "In mourning it is the world that has become poor and empty; in melancholia it is the ego itself." As if it were important to distinguish mourning from melancholy. But Freud seems to miss the crucial fact that one, when severe enough, necessarily becomes the other. We say "something inside me dies," but what we really mean is, if the world of my joy dies, then I must die with it. Not something inside me. Me. Mourning becomes melancholy, not Electra.

Which is why mourning's closest analogues are not sadness and depression but rather nostalgia and desire.

Nostalgia is from the Greek *nostos algos,* meaning the pain of returning home. Notice the sly doubleness of meaning in the idea of nostalgia, too often lost in our use of the word but worth bringing back into play. Nostalgia is homesickness at the level of a disease, the pain of one's longing to return. But nestled within its etymology is the coiled opposite, the pain of one's returning home, the jarring dislocations and inarticulate grievings of coming back, to something that is no longer as you imagined it during the homeward journey. This is a form of what our less-attuned age likes to call *culture shock,* only now both self-inflicted and self-reflexive.

Odysseus, perhaps the most famous nostalgic in Western literature, knew both sides of this pain: both the heartsick desire to return home, and the sagging awareness that the home he left is gone forever. Penelope is still there, to be sure, and the dog Argos knows him, and no one can bend the famous bow but him; and yet, everything is changed, everything lost, nothing can be recaptured. It's true: you really can't go home again.

Odysseus's scar is our scar too, and this is a weal that does not fade. Not even time, that celebrated physician, can heal such a wound. Nostalgia's desire, like mourning's loss, cannot be amended. Why? Because both function by definition: they are structurally inscribed as permanent, necessary, within the meanings of the words themselves. They are all about wanting what we cannot have. Our wanting is itself the indicator of impossibility, the sign of a necessary failure. It is more the goneness of what is gone than the whatness of what is gone that lays us low. People tell you this as if it were news, as if it will help—but you know it already and it doesn't. On the contrary. Yet once more, *that is the point.*

Holidays are bad. So are certain dishes of food, street signs, recreational activities, lines of poetry, photographs, movies, and pop songs. Some songs even seem to rub it in. Top of that list: Dionne Warwick reminding you that there is always something there to remind you.

Because there always is. The smell of sandalwood, the sound of Chet Baker's voice, Louise Brooks's haircut, walking in Central Park, skating in Nathan Phillips Square, kissing in St. James's Park.

You keep going over it, misremembering details and improving it and washing it with watercolour nuances and subtleties, the muted tones of romance. But you try to keep the other things too, for the sake of the larger truth of love's attachment: the tight shoes, the pimple, the looming deadlines, the myriad of mild irritations.

That helps. Sort of.

Work also helps. It is distracting, sometimes lucrative. It is, in almost every case, necessary. Most of all, it passes the time and so lifts the heavy weight of the pastness of the past. Work is also the only certain route away from resentment and bitterness, from the pain of loss, because it alone can create the accomplishments before which resentment loses its purchase. Boredom collapses in front of it.

But a lot of work is itself boring, and so becomes part of the problem rather than the solution. Working with other people should if possible be avoided, because other people, though not necessarily hell itself, now frequently seem to be annoying to the point of deserving death at your willing hands. They want things from you, they make demands, they behave as if nothing has changed. They get in the way.

So work by yourself if you can. Spend some time inside your own head. Get things done. Drink lots of coffee and remember to eat something before noon, maybe a bagel. Then, at about three in the afternoon, go to a movie. At about six, meet some like-minded people for a cocktail. Have two, then go somewhere for dinner. Talk of current events and professional jealousies. Discuss movies and books. Exchange gossip. Make artful allusions.

Go home, have a small nightcap, go to bed. That's enough. Avoid the temptation to perform any further self-medication. Do not indulge what Donne called the "sickly inclination" toward suicide, his own particular affliction.

And if you can, avoid the cycles of boredom and work altogether. Go fishing.

Mourning, like life more generally, is all about time. Time: the insuperable unidimensionality of it, its weird plasticity, the fact that sooner or later it ends for each of us. Living is a matter of filling in time with grace and wit, making good things and forging alliances with other prisoners of the temporal. Enjoying the things that are here, and that we have created for ourselves. Riding the wave of the present with as much wisdom and humour as you can muster, knowing so little about what is actually going on as you slide toward death.

Whatever else it is—brute existential fact, *a priori* form of sensibility, mere illusion—time is always the play of contingency and necessity. Living daily life in the routine hurries of time can obscure this, time the watched-clock enemy of ease, but reflecting on time in the timeless moments of angling's silence may allow the thought in. The contingency of time then often seems foremost. Who could know that you would both be there at that precise moment? Who could know that things would spark? Or that they would die? That love would die? That *he* or *she* would die?

So many possibilities! So many potential pathways branching out from the reality of that single moment.

But then the inevitable principle of necessity kicks in. Once taken, the path is not revisable. Alan Alda, in the film *Crimes and Misdemeanors,* says "comedy is tragedy plus time"—but that is not quite right. Nor was Marx correct when, chiding Hegel, he said that history always repeats itself, "the first time as tragedy, the second as farce." The hard truth is, rather, that comedy and tragedy are always twinned simultaneous possibilities, joined at the metaphysical hip, in the inescapable time-play of human life. *Oedipus the King* can be played as black comedy as well as tragedy, and the marriage-dance resolutions of Shakespeare's comedies can hide an encyclopedia of imminent woe. Miss that, and you miss the big picture.

You cannot be happy alone, and you cannot be happy together. Mourning mourns the loss of a possible future, the not-yet that now will never be. Everything ends, including you. Love is not eternal, it is not even hardy. Accepting this takes a form and amount of courage that nobody but you will see, or appreciate. You can't change any of this; you have to live with it. Is that funny or sad? You know that it is both, and neither. Once again—and as always—that is the point.

Irony helps. A little.

Get up. Begin. Make your way from the bed to the shower.

Remember that this is the hardest thing you will do all day.

We are out on the lake, Fred and I, in the boat on our last day of the trip, and it begins to rain, the light chop on the water rising to small frothy caps as dark grey clouds obliterate the once-beautiful day. The rain gets heavier and we decide to pack up. I haul the outboard to life and get us moving back across the open water.

It is now raining with intent, and the protected little corner of the lake, where fallen pines and a tiny cove have been coughing up the big fish all day, gives way to the windy open water. My body reminds me again that we are at more than four thousand feet above sea level and not far from the last frost. My hands on the tiller, wet from the lake, are growing frigid.

Without a word, Fred, facing me with his back to the prow, begins hauling foul-weather gear out of his hidden pockets and utility-belt compartments. He hands me a plastic slicker, which I quickly tug down over my shoulders; then, miraculously, a pair of woollen gloves with leather palms and fold-back tips. He seems to have extra hats and boots, maybe full-body camo outfits, stashed away on his Batman vest. We hunker down in the rain, slamming the boat over the small waves, heading in the general direction of the cabin, which I can now barely see past the sheets of rain.

In the manner of destinations across open water, especially in foul weather, the cabin seems to recede agonizingly even as we make our way toward it at full throttle, but finally we are within striking distance of the dock. I approach it with the little outboard engine wide open, then cut the gas suddenly in a way I love, just yards from the dock, so that the little craft glides smoothly into place alongside it on the surging backwash. We jump out, gather our beloved gear, and run up to the cabin. It is dark with clouds and nightfall, and we are completely drenched from the waist down, drowned rats in slickers and soaked ball caps.

My father, odd man out this time, has stayed behind in the cabin to read. But he has not been idle. A fire is roaring in the old iron wood stove, and the scotch bottle and glasses are set upon the table. There is beef stew simmering on the stove in the tiny kitchen and a couple of bottles of Montepulciano d'Abruzzo open to breathe. My father smiles at me as we cross the threshold of the cabin, the complicated imperfect smile of a not-quite-old man for his not-quite-middle-aged son.

I smile back. It's warm in there.